Play it my way

learning through play with your
visually impaired child

London: HMSO

Text © Royal National Institute for the Blind
224 Great Portland Street, London W1N 6AA
Tel: 0171-388 1266

First published 1995
ISBN 0 11 701676 4

Registered charity number 226227

Illustrations © Tony Harrison

Printed in the United Kingdom for HMSO
Dd300602 5/95 C20 G3397 10170

Contents

i

Chapter 3 – The space beyond me **47**

Foreword

Childhood should be fun for children and parents. Visual impairment should be no barrier to fun. This resource book for parents who are bringing up a visually impaired or multi-disabled visually impaired child contains a wealth of ideas based on practical experience. The activities suggested are easy to carry out in the course of day to day routines at home; many encourage imaginative use of everyday items around the house to help visually impaired children find out more about the world around them.

This is a book to dip into, and to refer to time and time again as your child grows, develops and explores. Your help is vital to ensure that your daughter or son **does** explore and get to know a world that is not clearly visible.

The play ideas, toys and materials have all been used successfully with visually impaired children who have multiple disabilities. Brothers and sisters with normal sight will enjoy them too. However, every child is an individual, and your child will let you know which activities are most enjoyable.

Making a start is often the hardest part, particularly if your child is slow to reward you with smiles and other signs of pleasure; we hope that these ideas for play and enjoyment will help you take those first steps. *Play it my way* is designed to give you the confidence to learn and play with a child who has a visual impairment, and to share in the excitement of each new experience.

Paul Ennals
Director
RNIB Education, Training and Employment Division

Acknowledgements

This book draws on the practical experience of parents, teachers and others involved in bringing up children who have impaired vision. Many people have contributed ideas for activities and play to supplement some of the ideas first generated by members of RNIB's team of education advisory teachers in the 1980s. Along the way, so many individuals have contributed to the content and helped to shape the structure of this book – our thanks are due to them all.

Special thanks go to Tina Bruce and Linda Pound, Centre for Early Childhood Studies, Roehampton Institute School of Education for guidance and ideas on early childhood development, and to April Winstock for advice on encouraging the development of eating and drinking skills. Thanks are due to Louise Clunies-Ross, Mary McDonald and Gill Pawley at RNIB for drafting, editorial and bibliographic input. Thanks also to Lis Grundy who provided many of the photographs for Tony Harrison's delightful drawings and to Kathy Rushton and Carol Lawrence who typed the manuscript.

Finally we would like to record our gratitude to HMSO for making these ideas more widely available by publishing this book.

Royal National Institute for the Blind
June 1995

Play it safe

The toys and materials mentioned in this book are simply a
starting point. You will discover new toys and games which
give particular pleasure to your child; equally a few toys may
go out of stock. However it is not so much **what** you play
with, but **how** you play, which will be important to your
child's development, curiosity and sense of fun.

Play it my way gives ideas to parents about play and
development activities. The originators shall not be liable for
any outcome associated with an activity suggested or any toy
or plaything recommended in this book. As with all children,
it is the responsibility of the parent or other adult in charge
(for example nursery leader or teacher) to ensure that
children's play activities all take place in a safe environment.

All the activities in this book are suitable for both girls and boys.
For ease of reading, we have used 'he' and 'she' in alternate
chapters.

Chapter 1

Who am I?

Introduction

Children with severe visual impairment

The different sections in this book emphasise individual aspects of helping children who have many learning difficulties as well as severe visual impairment. In practice, however, life is not so fragmented. Each aspect is inter-related and we find children using and developing various senses and skills together. The links between vision, movement, play, language and learning are explained to ensure greater understanding of the difficulties experienced from birth by children who have little or no sight.

In the following pages every area of development is touched upon. This is intended to be a resource book of ideas for parents to dip into and select the activities most suitable for their child. It is not a textbook or checklist! Rather it is a springboard for fun and games which, it is hoped, will be enjoyed by all the family. You may find you need to put aside a special time to carry out some of the play ideas while others fit naturally into normal routines.

Have fun!

It is so important to observe your child closely, as this occasion illustrates:

Lisa is totally blind, has cerebral palsy, and as yet does not have head control. She remained impassive at a visitor's attempt to play with her. However, her grandmother, who often cuddled and played with her, arrived and started to talk. Almost imperceptibly Lisa tilted her head very, very slightly in Gran's direction, started to vocalise and, barely noticeably, lifted one hand about three inches (75mm), repeating this every time Gran spoke. Unfortunately she was not facing the right way and Gran missed what, on that occasion, may have been an attempt to communicate, but the child's persistence suggested she was usually successful. In Lisa we see one of the many blind children with additional difficulties who have characteristics in common, but who are nevertheless special individuals, each with a unique personality.

Self-awareness, self-image and self-esteem

The sighted child

In everyday life we wear clothes to protect us from the elements. We build shelters for the same purpose. Through what we wear, the person who is clothed develops an image of SELF. But we are more than the clothes we wear. Who is the person underneath? Through becoming aware of our bodies, we develop a body image, which is part of our 'self'.

We do not exist in isolation from others. People live in relationships with others. Their home and the space beyond it are the ways young children develop an understanding of themselves in context.

A child begins to be aware of himself as he regards his fingers and toes, and realises they are part of him, which unlike his toys, cannot be lost. Through many ordinary experiences the growing child begins to be aware of:

- his own body and its different parts
- his body parts in relation to each other
- what he can do with his body whilst moving in various ways
- his body being separate from others
- how his own body is at any time in relation to things around him
- how other things are in relation to each other
- other people and how they feel about him
- how he can influence the world of people or objects by crying, talking, or using hands.

A child begins to learn about himself as a person with feelings and emotions, all of which are influenced by his abilities, the degree of success experienced, upbringing, the encouragement of one care-giver, and the skill of learning to control his body and its actions.

The visually impaired child

People who love and care are important to a visually impaired child, and they become very good at learning different ways to help that child.

At first this is difficult, especially when they are experiencing the deep emotional pain of adjusting to the child's special needs.

Visual impairment interferes with the development of self-image. Visually impaired children have fewer ways of observing what others are doing, of imitating and comparing themselves with their peers. In the absence of eye contact, facial expression and gesture, some people may not react normally to a child with a visual impairment. This, and a combination of other disabilities, can seriously impede their ability to be successful and to make necessary adjustments to their feelings about themselves, as we all have to do throughout life.

Visually impaired children use voice and touch.

At first this is difficult. As time goes on, parents will find themselves becoming sensitive to the special signals of their visually impaired child. He may not smile but 'still', as someone approaches or speaks. He may make inclinations of the head, quivery pleasure movements or vocalisations which, without eye contact, may not seem to be addressed to anyone. **These are all very real manifestations of a child's interest,** and he will need parents to respond with words or laughter, pleasant touch sensations, or varieties of movement, which can become quite energetic as the child becomes sturdier. Thus encouraged, a child may start to produce a richer repertoire of vocalisation and activity, and begin to show his own unique personality.

Partnership activities to encourage self-awareness

Here are some ideas to help your child have the sort of early experiences which will help awareness of self. Your child needs to

be handled – cuddle him, carry him around, so that he begins to be aware of 'self' and 'mum', or 'other special person' or 'other people'. At this point he really needs one person to relate to in a special way.

a   Play games on your lap, including rhythmical movements, like swaying, bouncing, rocking. Songs or rhymes which involve the body and end in a 'tickle', like 'Round and Round the Garden' are appropriate.

b   Blow gently, or blow 'raspberries' on his feet, hands, back, tummy, neck and ears.

c   Tickle his body all over with your fingers.

d   Brush all over his body with a soft brush.

e   Smooth his skin with the flat of your hands, using baby cream or light scented oil, or a light dusting of talcum powder.

f   Let him lie on the floor, in your arms with very few clothes on (especially remove socks), or in water. Give him the chance, at whatever stage of motor development he is, to feel his whole body against other people, or against surfaces. Make sure if he is fairly static, to vary his position and the surface –

carpet, linoleum, cushion, blanket, grass and so on. Make sure it is pleasant.

g In the bath gently play at sifting water over his shoulders, back, hands, and so on. When he is being dried, let him help you rub the towel over him, pat talcum powder onto his tummy, his feet, his arms and so on.

h If he hasn't naturally found his feet, touch them, name them, play with them, stroke them with a brush, on the soles, between the toes, over the arches, up his leg. Tickle and blow on his feet, then put his hands on them.

i Touch other parts of the body, name them and put his hands on each part.

j Sing lots of rhymes and songs involving touching parts of his body.

k Say 'Where is your hair?' (leg, arm, nose and so on). At first show him how to touch each as requested, but eventually expect him to do it on request.

l When your child is small and inactive, undress him, put some perfumed oil on your hands and spend a few minutes massaging all over his body bit by bit, naming his body parts.

m As he becomes more mobile, roll with him on the floor, let him climb over you and feel how your body is constructed, its size and how it moves. (Dads usually enjoy doing this.) Have him riding on your back as you crawl around or give him a pick-a-back. When he wants to be on his feet, walk with him on your toes.

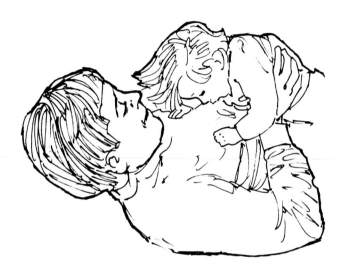

n Compare parts of the body, for example, 'Mum's foot', 'Jack's foot', or Mum's hair', 'Jack's hair', and so on.

Visually impaired children sometimes grow up without a complete awareness of the strength and power of their hands. Play games involving pulling and pushing, hugging and squeezing. (See Chapter 2 – Using hands.)

As everything your child does is helping him to develop his body image, all the other sections in this book should provide help for working with your child.

Using residual vision

The sighted child

In everyday life, sighted children build up an understanding and awareness of self. They develop self-esteem.

Children look at the world and those in it. Looking is important in learning about objects which are far away, or detailed because they are closer. Looking helps children to interpret the world, to be aware, to pay attention and to understand.

A baby born with normal sight learns to:

1   fix his gaze on something (fixate)

2   focus

3   shift his gaze from item to item

4   follow (or track) objects

5   maintain eye contact with people

The visually impaired child

Visually impaired children need special help in building up this understanding. Many visually impaired children have some residual vision which can be used if they are helped to learn to use it, but not all do.

If your child does not have residual sight, we suggest you move on to another part of the book.

Does your child stop an activity when reflected or coloured lights are shone near him?

Do your child's eyes flicker, or does facial expression change?

Does your child look towards lights and/or reflections?

Does your child seem to 'fixate' on your face even for a moment?

These are signs of some residual vision. Visually impaired babies need visually stimulating experiences which encourage the use of residual vision, so that **looking** becomes a more efficient aid to understanding the world. As a general rule, eye and brain are stimulated by things which contrast with the background. Things which wobble or rotate or make a sound help fixating to be held.

Partnership activities to encourage looking

a Prop a mirror in front of your child, so the mirror is facing away from the window.

b Shine a coloured torchlight on your child's face and move it vertically upwards, or horizontally in either direction. Red, deep purple, orange are often favourites. (Coloured acetate or cellophane comes in a range of deep and pale shades of primary colours.)

c Hold a visually attractive musical roundabout or similar toy near the line of vision and move it horizontally or vertically.

d When your child is lying on his back, put a visually attractive toy on his chest, hoping this will encourage him to tilt his head and look.

e Use a torch with a coloured acetate or cellophane in deep red, purple, orange, yellow, green and blue to attract your child's attention. Note which colours the child shows awareness of and turn the light onto your face, your hands, and your child's hands and feet. Use two colours to begin with, adding another when you feel the child is sufficiently aware and responsive to this game until all colours have been used extensively.

A progression of this game is to shine the coloured lights onto a pale wall, moving them both horizontally and diagonally, slowly, to encourage a child to 'track' by placing his hands or fingers on the 'dancing light'.

A further progression would be for him to use his feet to step on the coloured lights.

f Fix a shiny foil windmill near your child in a place where it can be spun easily by a passer-by.

g Suspend foil Christmas decorations from a coat hanger on thin hat elastic of different lengths, so that sunlight catches the rich colours of the foils on this mobile to attract your child's attention. These are good to touch as well as to look at and when the elastic is pulled gently, the foil decorations make soft sounds as they move and bounce together.

h A variety of shatterproof shiny Christmas decorations can be fastened together in a bunch to suspend on elastic, or to attach to the side of a child's cot or chair. These make an interesting sound when the elastic is tweaked and are excellent attention-catchers when the sun or some other bright light shines on them.

i Look out for colourful fish, flower, or other mobiles, made from shells which allow light to shine through as well as produce interesting sounds.

j String a wide length of elastic across a child's cot from side to side, hung with items such as a couple of shiny dessert spoons on a ribbon, shatterproof or foil decorations, large glass beads or perspex cotton reels on a ribbon, a child's shatterproof mirror, a brightly coloured rattle, coloured transparent bracelets strung on elastic ribbon, a Kiddicraft 'Wobble Globe' hung upside down. Each is fascinating to young children.

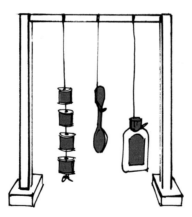

k Place a large, brightly coloured, inflatable toy, or a weighted wobbly man beside your child as he lies or sits. Remember to move it to the opposite side often so that he learns to turn to focus on objects on either side, if this is possible for him. Physical disability may restrict his movements for this, but any movement the child makes will cause the wobbly man to bob about and bounce back. If the facial features are clear and distinctive your child will be encouraged to maintain eye contact with the toy's face.

l There are many 'fibre-optic' lamps available now in addition to inexpensive 'bear' night lamps for children. The latter are easily found and have a switch which can easily be touched as you pass by to light up the pink or yellow 'bear', or to put out the light so that the child begins to wait and look for it.

m Place assorted mobiles in different rooms in your house. This also helps your child to associate different sounds with places.

n Knit yourself a pair of gloves with different coloured fingers and waggle your coloured fingers in front of your child to draw his attention as you speak to him. One-size novelty 'magic gloves' are very useful for this activity.

o Suspend a noise-making toy, such as a chirping bird with real feathers, on a spring above where your child lies or sits. Whenever you pass, touch the spring to set the bird in motion again.

p Attach brightly coloured cellophane or acetate squares to your windows or to glass panels in doors around the house, but especially near where your child sits. These are interesting when the sunlight shines through them and are good to encourage exploration and experimentation with colour when objects outside are looked at through the plain glass and through cellophane or acetate. Give your child some coloured cellophane or acetate to handle, or cover your face or hands with it to play a version of 'peek-a-boo'.

Eye contact with a person

When people communicate, they look at each other and establish eye contact.

The visually impaired child

During caring routines, people a child loves have many opportunities to encourage eye contact, especially when a mother talks to her child and moves closer to him and away a little – gradually increasing the distance until eye contact with the child is lost.

Partnership activities to encourage eye contact with a person

a   Wear coloured spectacle frames sometimes when playing with your child.

b   Put on a brightly coloured hat (or a patchwork tea-cosy!) to help your child to look at, and pay more attention to you.

c   Wear a 'disco-hat' with flashing lights to encourage your child to establish eye contact with you. Follow this up with the child wearing the disco-hat as he looks at his image in a mirror before him.

d   Wear a false red sponge nose yourself and move your head up and down or from side to side. Similarly, wear a colourful funny hat – add a big bright feather – and, later, use a bright colourful mask for peek-a-boo games with your child.

e   Make paper plate faces with different distinctive features – use one as a mask for peek-a-boo games and suspend others on your child's cot, chair or table and in other rooms of the house.

f   Put on a foil 'wig'. See if he looks up to your hairline.

g Place a red sponge ball or coloured matchbox on your nose or wear a false beard or moustache as you face and play with your child. Move away and then close again until you are sure that he is maintaining eye contact with you.

h Use face paints (Galt and Early Learning Centre make these) to highlight your facial features.

i Emphasise your eyes and lips with extra heavy eye shadow and very bright lipstick.

j Wear a bright mask and call his name as you peer at him through the eye mask.

A more formal approach may be to sit opposite your child and hold something he likes at the bridge of your nose. If he looks at your eyes, give him the object to encourage him. It should be remembered that some children see best at an angle, and your child may have to tilt his head to look at your eyes. Some children may have useful vision in one eye only.

Eye contact with an object

Looking at objects is an important way of learning for all children.

The visually impaired child

This skill is important in developing hand-eye coordination. If your child seems to have some residual vision, present objects within your child's line of vision and encourage reaching and grasping. Don't put objects into your child's hands. Encourage your child to take them from you, and develop the ability to 'look'.

Partnership activities to encourage eye contact with objects

a Use a Jack-in-the-box to attract your child's attention – encourage him to press Jack's head to make him disappear, then give verbal clues such as, 'Watch! Jack's coming again!'

b A musical, brightly coloured merry-go-round is very useful for helping a child to maintain eye contact with an object.

c A colourful clockwork toy which moves on the spot, such as a yellow fluffy chicken, may be fascinating for a child to fixate on.

d Flicker a torchlight with a coloured filter in front of the child's eyes, or to one side or the other from different distances for several seconds at a time. See how long he can maintain fixation with it. Notice if he has colour preferences.

e Hold a bicycle reflector steady a short distance from his eyes and flicker a torchlight behind it. See in which direction he is best able to maintain eye contact with it.

f Holograph stickers are fascinating when used with a torch or other light source to intensify colours and give 3-d pictures.

g See if your child will fixate on a toy with a flashing light or a beacon.

h Look for small scented candles in a tin which smell good when lit. Encourage your child to **watch** the flickering flame, **feel** the heat, **smell** the wax and **blow out the candle**. (Supervise closely to be sure that he cannot burn himself if he reaches out to touch the candle.)

i Your child will enjoy watching a home-made 'diffractive' spinner or a commercially available 'dimension disc' when this toy is spun beneath a bright light to intensify the hidden colours in the spinner. Use a torch so that the spinner with its deep colours can be really close to him.

j Reflective shapes (normally used on cars and bicycles) make good spinning toys with a diffractive effect when threaded on plastic covered garden wire with beads to separate the pieces. This will encourage your child to watch the movements and to try to spin the toy himself with some success.

k Fireworks and sparklers are fun for your child to watch.

l A Christmas decoration in which Santa's face can be clipped to a support, encourages looking, as his face lights up and his nose glows red when the string is pulled.

m Glow-balls, 'neon' laces, luminous moon, star and arrow mobiles are all excellent toys for encouraging tracking in a dimly lit room. These items need to be held under a bright light for several minutes before use. They glow for some time, depending on the intensity of the light used.

Looking and reaching

Swiping at objects encourages children to watch the movement and reach out for the object again. All children track objects and people as they look at them moving.

The visually impaired child

Children begin 'swiping' at things, and moving their hands to try to touch things they see in an uncoordinated way. Look at 'Swiping and swishing' section in Chapter 2 for some activities that will help your child to track objects and people as they move.

Partnership activities to encourage your child to track objects

a   Use a colour torch. Get your child's attention with it by putting the colour **near** to his eyes, but **not** directly into his eyes. Move away a little, still keeping his visual attention, then move the light slowly from side to side, from one side to the other, then up, down and diagonally. As soon as you lose his attention, move the torch closer to him again. Repeat this at increasing distances until you have some idea of the distance ('visual field') where the child cannot follow the movements and is presumably unable to see the torchlight. Repeat this with other colours. You will find out if his sight is stronger at one side than the other.

b   Hold a brightly coloured toy (purple, red and orange are good colours) in front of your child at midline – move it across his line of vision horizontally, vertically or in a circle. If he is at the stage of reaching out then put the toy within his arm's length so that he can touch or grasp it. **His visual impressions have a more concrete meaning for him if he can touch the toy in this way.** Whilst he is engrossed in looking at the toy, occasionally produce another shiny toy or torchlight from his side, moving it very slowly forwards towards the midline to try to distract him.

c   Talking to your child and helping him to maintain eye contact during caring routines has been mentioned elsewhere. Now is the time for you to talk to your child as you move about the room to give him a **verbal clue as well as a visual one**.

d   Encourage him to watch clockwork toys moving at different speeds and in varying directions on a table or tray before him. These are now available in a range of sizes – large and small pecking or hopping birds, dogs with spinning tails, dogs which turn somersaults, Paddington Bears or Noddy which move forward at a steady pace, ladybirds which go round in circles, aeroplanes which perform 'loop the loop' actions, 'walking shoes', moving teapots whose lids move up and down and so on. All are readily obtainable at toyshops, newsagents and chemists.

e   Encourage your child to focus his attention on a car racing track, train set, or on a 'penguin on the escalator' toy. Similarly, any toys which involve tracking rolling balls or marbles such as bagatelle, snooker, helter skelter and so on are very useful at this stage.

f   Help him to blow bubbles and to watch and try to catch them as they float about him.

g   Roll a brightly coloured ball towards him. If he is capable of some mobility, encourage him to participate. With frequent practice this will develop into a real ball game – perhaps one day he will be tempted to pick up the ball to throw it or maybe kick it.

h   A brightly coloured toy pulled along the floor in front of a child, or a 'melody train' toy that moves in ever-widening circles, can be interesting to him at this stage although he may not want to 'pull' the train with you.

i   Look for a 'woodpecker on a tree' type toy, where the bird springs up and down as he pecks his way from the top of the 'tree' to the bottom. This toy is good for encouraging up and down tracking.

j   A 'Humpty on a ladder' toy can be made at home or perhaps borrowed from the local toy library. Your child will need to look up to the top of the ladder to watch 'Humpty' wobble from side to side down to the bottom.

k   Buy a 'tacky octopus' – a small soft plastic octopus with long, thin tentacles, all of which are 'tacky' to touch. Place the octopus on a mirror or window and encourage your child to watch it as the toy slowly moves down the glass, somersaulting all the way.

l   'Magic wands' (fibre-optic torch) with their glowing tips are very popular and useful aids in helping with visual stimulation. Wave a wand in a dimly lit room to encourage your child to track its movements. This is light enough for even 'floppy' hands to manipulate so the child can safely wave this about and watch both the glowing dots and his own hand movements. Use it also when it is beginning to get dark outside, so that the light and patterns made by the wand are reflected in the window panes.

m   Toys which have flashing lights and movement, such as robots, beacons and UFOs are interesting and visually stimulating.

n   Sparklers are fun for a child to watch if you move them in circles.

o All kinds of Chinese/Japanese paper decorations are **interesting to touch** as well as to watch them 'grow' into lanterns, flowers, colourful circles and so on, from their flat state.

p A 'Jumping Jack' toy, a figure whose limbs are linked together by a pull-cord, jumps with moving arms and legs when the string is **pulled**. This is a useful toy which can be hung on a child's cot or above him, on a frame, as he sits in his chair or beanbag.

q Use a selection of brightly coloured plastic swans or other inflatable toys in the bath or a shallow bowl. There are wind-up toys also, frogs and fish of various colours, sizes and speed of movement. Your child may be stimulated to watch and try to catch them.

r Collect empty, transparent poster tubes, or button tubes from a haberdashery department or shop and use these with various sizes of cake and trifle decoration balls, or with a marble or hazelnut or walnut in its shell to encourage your child to **shake**, or **tip from side to side**, causing the contents to slide. These tubes are good for helping **left to right eye movements**, **two handed activity** and for **feeling the vibration** and **weight** of the cake decorations, marbles or nuts as they slide or roll.

s When your child has had practice in tracking and, we hope, handling some of the toys mentioned above, begin to extend his tracking and hand-eye coordination by using a torch and coloured acetate, to play a game of 'dancing fingers'. Draw the curtains to darken the room and encourage him to watch patches of coloured light shone on a wall – moving vertically, diagonally, and horizontally. Ask him to make his fingers 'dance' on the coloured patches. Shone on the floor he may like to touch with his feet or move to the light.

t Magnetic frogs, ladybirds and balls are available in toy and joke stores. Use these to create more 'magic' for your child by placing one of a pair of frogs on top of a wooden tray and draw the other one along underneath the tray. The frog on top will move forward or spin in response to the hidden magnetic toy. There are many other small magnetic toys which can be used in a similar way but on top of the tray or table – for example a sea lion and ball, cat and mouse, in which the ball spins as it moves away from the sea lion and the mouse moves until suddenly the cat 'pounces'. These are fun to use and require the child to track small items moving about closer to him than some of the toys mentioned elsewhere in this section.

u   Use a variety of coloured beanbags of different weights (paper, rice, peas, buttons) on your child's head, hands and feet. Encourage him to tilt his head, shake his hands, waggle his feet, to remove these beanbags and see if he looks to find out where they have gone.

Chapter 2

Using hands

Introduction

How sighted children use their hands

During the very early weeks of life, a baby's hands may be closed, with thumbs turned in, perhaps opening out if she extends her arms. Normally, a baby's reflex to grasp an object touching her palm will have ceased before three months, giving way for the development of purposeful grasp.

However, the rate of progress through the following stages depends greatly on the child's maturing nervous system.

1   She is excited at the sight of objects.

2   She starts to 'swipe' at them with increasing activity.

3   She scoops in a nearby object with her arm for a closer look.

4   She brings her hands together and plays with her fingers in front of her eyes.

5   She holds an object put into her hand and may bring it to her face.

6   Later, she looks at the object.

7   She looks at her hand and the object.

8   She starts to reach out with her hands to grasp things she sees.

9   She practises reaching and with increasing accuracy. Seeing helps a child to direct her reach and control her grasp.

Visually impaired children

Although visually impaired children may not be able to see their hands or objects they could hold in them, they can be helped to use their hands as an important way of learning.

Your child

Visually impaired children may need particular help but this will depend upon hearing, residual vision, additional disabilities, general development and the things they like doing.

When you start to encourage your child to use her hands you may find that she seems unaware of them and will need help to notice them. Children do gradually become aware that they have hands and you can help your child with this.

When a child has some vision, hand regard should be encouraged. This will help the child to develop hand-eye coordination, and swiping movements, with hand and object. They begin to judge their relationship more accurately. Even if there is no vision, it is important for your child to play with her fingers and to learn to reach out, grasp objects and judge where objects will be.

You can use this next section to 'pick and mix' activities, and see what appeals to your child and you together.

Your child may not seem to care for physical contact, or like having her hands touched. This may be more common in premature babies or those who have spent time in hospital. Such children will need short and frequent opportunities to learn to enjoy contact with a familiar adult. You will need to explore the range of activities suggested to find which ones appeal and which ones do not. Your child may show fear of new objects. **Don't reject an activity because your baby doesn't respond on one occasion**. Look for any sign of pleasure. Small movements of hands, arms or feet, as well as in facial expression, may show you that your child is enjoying the activity.

There may be physical limitations. A child's hands, for example, may be tightly clenched. Difficulties in bringing hands together or raising arms may be helped in various ways. A child who has cerebral palsy, for example, who is lying on her back may need to have head and shoulders resting on a pillow. Shoulders will then be brought forward causing the arms and hands to be more relaxed.

Try to find the best position for your child. Prop her up in a sitting position on the floor, very well supported by cushions. These will be less necessary as she gains in sitting balance. A physiotherapist may suggest special seating when she is at floor level. If she suggests something to bring her higher, she will probably need support for her feet. If your child has some vision, she will have a better chance to observe the movement of familiar people and making social contact when she is in a sitting position.

Regular changes of position and place give variety to her experience and help to keep her alert.

Sometimes a child might benefit from having her toes and perhaps much of her body bare, to feel the surface she is lying on, the hands and clothes of the people who tend her, the air wafting in through the window, freedom to kick without encumbrance and be better able to appreciate the pressures on her skin as she is cuddled, tickled, turned and lifted.

Partnership activities to encourage hand awareness

a   Massage your child's hands, individually and together, perhaps with baby lotion or perfumed oil. Caress her hands, trying to make them as relaxed and supple as possible.

b   Blow on her hands. Bring the baby's palms to your face. Touch them, name them, play with them, stroke them with a brush, tickle them. Some babies enjoy having 'raspberries' blown on their hands.

c   Touch the palms of your baby's hand with your hand, or with an appropriately sized object. In very young babies this may cause a reflex grasp.

d   Where there is residual vision, a band of diffractive material attached to each hand might enable the baby to notice her hands. Move the hands individually or together, close to her eyes. Alternatively, mittens might have diffractive or sequinned materials stuck onto them.

e   Brush your child's hand with a variety of materials such as brushes, nylon scourer, velvet, corduroy, pumice, sponge, dish mop, feathers, towels, talc, sugar, honey, or marmite.

f   Gently shaking your child's arm from the elbow, or stroking the back of the hand or forearm will help her to relax her hand and open it out.

g   Tickle the hands while reciting any rhymes or songs you know. 'Round and Round the Garden' or 'This Little Piggy' are old favourites but you may prefer to make up your own. Notice and encourage responses which indicate a readiness for more goes.

Songs and finger rhymes have a special part to play in helping children to develop language and awareness of their bodies.

Looking at hands

All children

Before children reach out accurately for a toy, they go through a period of looking at their hands, making patterns with their fingers.

Visually impaired children

We need to encourage this in our children. Playing hand and finger games, blowing, tickling and stroking helps them to pay attention to hands. In other sections of this book there are ideas for making 'glitter' mittens, 'interest' gloves and interest bags and purses. At this point the concern is to make your child aware of her own hands as part of her self-image.

Partnership activities to encourage looking at hands

a   Shine a coloured light onto her hands. Put one of her hands in the torchlight and make a silhouette.

b   Use the 'interest' bags (see page 27) on her hands to enable her to watch and exercise her fingers, and to remind your child that she has **two** hands.

c   Sew small bells (from craft and pet shops) on to 25mm/one-inch wide elastic to fit round her wrists and ankles, neither too tightly nor too loosely. As she moves, these will help to draw her attention to hands and feet.

d Use colourful finger puppets, coloured cellotape, or face paints (Galt or Early Learning Centre), on her fingertips and nails – this will help her to look purposefully at her hands.

Swiping and swishing

All children

Children begin to reach out and swipe and swish at objects.

Visually impaired children

If, as your child's hands move accidentally, they touch hanging objects which feel or sound interesting, her movements may become more purposeful. Remember, however, it may be necessary to show her how to knock a hanging object.

Your child will need help and encouragement to sweep in a nearby object with her arm for a closer look and feel.

Partnership activities to help your child to swipe and swish

It is useful to have a heavy based frame or dress rail, or a broom handle firmly tied between two dining chairs. If you have a frame for a baby gym, it can serve the same purpose. To any one of these a number of attractive objects can be suspended on elastic at varying heights to encourage your child to fixate on, reach to knock, to grasp, to pull, to push or to shake.

a **A bamboo mobile** can easily be made at home. Cut even lengths of garden canes with one 'notch' in each. Drill a hole through the middle and thread a string through. Tie a large knot to prevent it slipping through. Tie it to a bamboo crossbar. Six or seven lengths of this make a beautiful sound. Polish each piece of bamboo with sandpaper to ensure that there are no jagged ends; varnish each section if you wish.

b **A shatterproof mirror** – again suspended on elastic so that it spins.

c   **A brightly coloured (home-made) feather duster** on a length of dowelling rod. Suspend with elastic. Buy packs of different coloured feathers to make a really fluffy duster.

d   **Shatterproof Christmas decorations** fastened together and suspended by approximately 30 cm/12 inches. They come in different sizes, shapes and colours, sparkle in bright light, and make a rewarding tinkling sound as they move.

e   **Slinky spring** - a great favourite with many uses.

f   **Metal or plastic shiny or coloured bracelets** strung on elastic.

g   **A string of brass or silver bells** with a curtain ring attached by a chain or bright ribbon. Encourage your child to put her fingers into the curtain ring and move it to set the bells ringing. The child is rewarded for very little effort.

h   **Clear plastic or perspex beads, cotton reels, and large and small bells** strung on plastic covered garden wire or electrical cable.

i   **Balloons** – partly inflated, with rice or peas inside make a pleasant sound if touched.

j   **A bicycle horn** to be squeezed by a passer-by to regain the child's attention.

k   **A net bag** containing unshelled nuts.

l   **A net bag** containing different sizes of balls.

Look around the house; there are many other interesting objects there which can be used in this way to 'ring the changes', and keep your child curious and stimulated. Helpful toys to put before children at this stage are those which have beads and bobbles on springs, for example a bobbly musical box or a Clatterpillar with its antennae with beads which spring back. A child should have an array of toys within easy reach on her tray, or on the floor around her.

Touch switches can often be attached to battery operated toys, lights, and so on and reward a child for her efforts.

Colourful lightweight balls fastened with stalks of florists' wire to a solid block of wood, bobble about and knock together with the slightest touch.

Further suggestions of objects to hang on mobiles to be swiped at include:

- shells
- bamboo pieces
- ceramic pieces
- brass bells
- spoons
- rattles
- feathers
- an old talc tin
- shatterproof and foil Christmas decorations
- cotton reels
- balloons
- slinky spring
- a bar of soap in a net
- plastic bracelets
- an old jiffy lemon
- lavender bag
- beanbag
- dish mop

Try holding a large tin lid behind so that it acts like a gong as the mobile hits it.

Look out for blow-up toys which squeak when hit and return to an upright position after they have been swiped at.

In addition, a 'swipe' over the bobbles of a **Kouvalios** musical box starts the tune off momentarily.

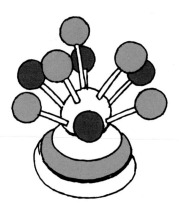

Have a variety of shallow containers around such as a cardboard box, biscuit tin, or a wooden or tin tray. Experiment with different contents. Help her to learn to 'swish' or 'scoop' objects like cotton reels, corks, large beads, varieties of balls, large buttons, an old chain belt, off-cuts of wood, clothes pegs, rice, lentils, sand or cornflakes. This may be a good activity when your child is on her tummy over a roll or a wedge.

Touching and holding objects

All children

All children have quiet moments when they touch things with their hands and just 'mess about', holding objects. With sighted children this can happen 'naturally'.

Visually impaired children

Always have some objects which can be touched or which your child can close her hands around and hold.

Partnership activities to help your child to touch and hold objects

a Introduce **'interest' bags**, perhaps made of net, attached by velcro, or elastic garters, or ribbons, to the inside of her palm for her fingers to feel and grasp – the bag may contain milk bottle tops, polystyrene chips, sweet smelling mixed herbs, lavender, nuts in shells, large buttons, corks, wood shavings, scrunchy paper, a bunch of keys, or a bunch of shatterproof decorations.

b Put one of her hands inside an interest bag and tie it around her wrist, hoping her fingers will grasp at the contents.

c Put a piece of paper into one of her hands and close her fingers around it.

d Thread a ribbon through a fairly large bead. Place the bead into her palm and secure with velcro.

e At this stage arm movements may be very limited, so you can dress her in a bib, vest or jacket, to which is attached a variety of interesting objects to scratch at or grasp. To keep alive your child's curiosity it is good to change the items. An easy way to do this is to tie them onto curtain rings which are firmly stitched to the garment.

f She may have started a little exploratory feeling and scratching on surfaces or gathering in toys with a sweep of her arms and hands. Whether she is lying down or sitting supported it is an idea for your child to have at hand's reach, surfaces or objects to scratch and grasp at such as a raffia mat, shiny survival blanket, flat cardboard box, corduroy, corrugated card, biscuit paper, paper, boxed wine containers. You may think of other ideas. A handy relative may be persuaded to sew you a mat with interesting tactile surfaces.

g Put bells on to 15mm/half inch wide elastic garter or strip of velcro and attach this to her wrists, so that any movement of her hands or wrist will shake the bells. (These can also be used on a child's ankles.)

h After a verbal warning, touch the back of one of her hands with a gentle vibrating device. Move it over the rest of her hand. Put it into her palm. Bring the other hand over to it.

i Push a quoit or plastic slinky spring or bracelet up her arm as far as her elbow. This may provoke a response of some sort as she tries to get it off by shaking her arm or using the other hand or her mouth to get rid of it. If she cries, gently show her how to release the bracelet with the other hand.

j Whilst she is bathing, pour water over her hands, or rub them in soapy bubbles. Also try using brightly coloured bath paints.

k Have bags of small objects such as buttons or rice. Put both her hands inside and rub them together whilst feeling the bag's contents.

Look particularly for things which make unusual sounds or have interesting textures, such as vivid rubber pom-poms called Koosh balls. Look too for different examples of the same things such as spoons, brushes and so on.

Bringing hands together

Hand regard and finger play

Bringing hands together is important and visually impaired children often need encouragement to do so. They will need help to learn how to use two hands together for delicate manipulative activities. Where sight is normally used to refine a movement, the hands must learn to work in unison in a well coordinated fashion. Many self-help activities require this. A visually impaired child who is physically disabled down one side of her body, needs to use her poor hand as a support and clamp, whilst her good hand makes the finer movements.

When a child has even the slightest bit of vision, hand regard should be encouraged. If she has no vision she can still play with her own fingers and begin to learn to reach out to grasp objects, and to make judgements about where objects she has put down will be found.

When you think your child has some vision:

a   Put a 'collar' of diffractive material around each hand. Move each hand individually and together close to her eyes.

b   Put 'glitter' mittens on her, ones with diffractive material stuck on fingers and palms, or made of sequinned material.

c   Put 'interest' gloves or mittens on her, for example gloves with shiny buttons and bells on the fingers, and perhaps squeakers in the palms. Help her to discover the interesting sounds which are made by bringing hands together and clapping. A perfumed bag attached to the back of a glove adds further interest.

Whether a child has vision or not:

d   Play 'pat-a-cake', moving her hands for her if necessary.

e   Get a large ball of paper and help her squeeze it between both her hands.

f   Play 'pat-a-cake' with a slinky spring attached over both wrists. It produces a nice 'click' as her hands are brought together.

Encouraging purposeful grasping

Children begin to feel things they want to grasp. They reach out for them on purpose.

Introduce your child to things which have a variety of appeal such as an interesting shape, a reflecting or colourful surface, interesting texture, something with holes in, things with different types of sound potential when shaken, banged, tapped, scratched, rubbed and so on.

Help your child to enjoy grasping things, and give a rich variety of experiences to her. Always look out for signs of what your child finds interesting.

Partnership activities that encourage grasping

a   Paper – let her experiment with varieties that 'scrunch' when grasped.

b   Using a medium-sized bead with a ribbon through, put the bead in her hand, the ribbon through her fingers, and pull slightly.

c   A battery-operated toothbrush – take some of the weight by holding the wide end yourself. Close her fingers around the brush as it vibrates.

d   Make a strong 'bracelet' of 15mm/half inch beads and elastic. Fit it over her palm and close her hand.

e   Make a strong string of 15mm/half inch beads, 150mm/ 6 inches long, and with a bell on the end. Close her hand around it and move her hand to show that it shakes or scrapes along surfaces with an interesting sound.

f   Put a plastic slinky spring into her hand. Show how it clicks when shaken and has an interesting feel as it moves. Hang it over her hand, hoping her hand will close around it.

g   Some of the 'interest' bags can be used again at this point for one- and two-handed grasping, especially those which make a sound when handled.

h   Children find the bobbles on a 'bobbly' musical box exciting to touch because they click together or the music begins to play. Often a child will close her hand around the springy antennae.

i   Put velcro 'dart balls' onto a toy felt dartboard or tin lid covered in felt. They are fun to grasp and pull off.

k   Alternatively, stick the dart ball on your child's clothing for her to grasp and pull off.

l   Make a 'twizzle stick' from 230mm/9 inches of dowelling with strips of metallic looking shiny coloured wrapping paper attached to each end. When the child holds the middle of the stick and moves or shakes it, the paper rustles, and also flashes for those with some sight. (Blu-tack in the middle of the stick helps those who find grasping difficult.)

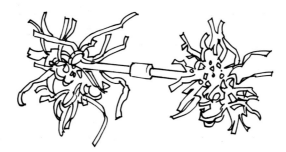

This selection of 'toys' will sometimes motivate those children who may otherwise be reluctant to explore objects with their hands, so that they begin to feel, to shake, to bang, to 'mouth', to scratch, tap, rub, turn over, to put hands or fingers through, to poke, bite, smell, drop, listen, as well as to seek and scan for other objects in their environment. Variety is the spice of life! It may be necessary to **show** your child **how** to play in these ways.

These activities will help your multi-disabled visually impaired child to have the means to learn to play imaginatively. We should remember that the key to the world about her lies in her hands and in her hearing – and this does not just **happen**. Your child needs help to move into play.

A list of materials which are interesting to handle:

- knitting machine cones (variety of size, shape and colour)
- palm-sized home-made shakers from suitable empty containers
- a number of plastic curtain rings strung on elastic
- squeezy lemon bottle
- hair rollers strung on ribbon
- musical (tinkly) toothbrush
- cotton reels strung on ribbon
- plastic or wooden finger rings strung out on elastic are good for poking fingers through
- craft shops are a good source for varieties of beads, rings, toggles, bamboo pieces, squeakers, handles, fancy textures of ribbons and cords
- soap on a rope
- loofah on a rope
- Blu-tack to squeeze
- lavender bag
- dough to squeeze
- small handbell
- musical toy dumb-bell

Reaching out for objects

Sighted children begin to reach out for objects that they see and want to hold, or swipe or swish at. They relate three things; sound, sight and touch, and associate them with an object.

A visually impaired child must be prompted to reach beyond herself. As she learns to move, she actively learns about new things in her immediate environment. Remember that her understanding of language, too, will be restricted to her experience.

Although reaching is particularly difficult for some visually impaired children if there is the added complexity of physical disabilities, a child can begin to understand that there are exciting things 'out there' to reach for.

The following activities will help your child to begin understanding that an object makes sounds, has a particular texture and looks a particular shape. Until your child has begun to explore them, sounds will simply be something to listen to.

Activities to encourage your child to reach out for objects

a Keep a frame of interesting hanging objects but do be careful to see that they are safe to play with if put in the child's mouth.

b Put sound-making objects at arm's length in front of your child:
- brass desk bell
- touch switches attached to battery operated toys

- 12-tune musical door bell. (The small press button switch may be too small for some children. It may be necessary to replace with a touch switch.)
- folded up survival blanket
- scrunchy paper
- wobbly toy to knock
- peek-a-boo roller
- children's night light
- wobble ball
- musical merry-go-round
- silver inner bag from a wine box

c   Surround your child with a great variety of interesting objects, whether she is sitting or lying. Try to ensure that each object has a knob, a stem, a hole or dent or antenna which makes it easy to hold with a palmar grasp or hooked finger.

d   At this stage we do not first put things into a child's hand, but prompt her by touching the back of her hand with it, saying, 'Here you are'.

Reaching up and out

Sighted children see things at different levels, low and high, and at eye level. They reach up for them, or out or down. Children begin to look ahead, reach down for their feet, out at their shoulder level, on either side, up above their heads, and behind their backs.

Your child needs help in understanding that things can be found at different levels and not just on the floor or in a tray in front of her. Moreover, many things will not fit into one hand, but may still be handled despite their size and weight. You may need to stretch your arms around to support or hold some of them.

We must therefore consciously create opportunities for a visually impaired child to begin to stretch her arms and trunk.

Remember that a visually impaired child needs to learn to be curious about her surroundings.

Helping your child to reach up and out

For example:

a   She may well be motivated to stretch her arms around a large teddy to cuddle it if teddy vibrates or talks.

b   Patting a balloon or a large inflatable shape hung above her head is a game she can share with others in the family, providing good social contact.

c   When Dad asks 'Do you want a swing?' your child becomes accustomed to stretching up towards her father's hands ready to begin this pleasurable activity.

d   Let her stretch out on the stairs and support her well.

e   Let her stand to feel the top of the table or the edge of the settee, or touch a door knob, light switch, or bell. Some children need to be encouraged and helped to do this.

Two-handed play

Sighted children begin to change an object from hand to hand. At this early stage a visually impaired child is more likely to scan around with one hand, with sweeping movements, and grasp whatever her hand touches. It is important to encourage **two-handed play**, leading to the long term objective of enabling a child to progress as far as possible in acquiring those skills necessary for eating, washing face and hands, dressing, bathing, and washing hair and clothes.

In this section, we look at ways to encourage your child to develop two-handed play.

Long objects, such as sticks with bells on, or a stiff cord with beads threaded on it, or medium-sized plastic rings joined together, or long ropes of objects, or a slinky spring, are appropriate toys, as well as many others already mentioned. You may have to show your child how to transfer things from one hand to the other as well as encourage her verbally.

The hand to mouth stage will be developing, encouraged by interesting tastes and smells on the fingers. At this stage, we expect a child to use her mouth as well as her hands to explore objects, so playthings will have to be safe for this kind of investigative play.

Put interesting flavours, textures of food, and smells on her fingers such as marmite, peanut butter, chocolate, ice cream, honey, jam, coffee. The long term objective is, first, finger feeding and later, spoon feeding herself.

Dropping and tactile scanning

Children begin to look for objects they have dropped. As far as she is concerned, when a visually impaired child reaches the stage where she drops her toys, they may well have disappeared completely. Gently put her hand on the dropped toy, or return it to her. When she is actively engaged in tactile scanning and retrieving, this will lead on, when she is much older, to the more sophisticated technique of:

a   listening to the direction where the object has dropped, and

b learning to move her fingertips outwards from her body in small circles on the surface (for example the floor or table) in the direction of the sound until location of the object is achieved.

Your child might be obsessed with this activity. Many multi-disabled children are. This is because:

a the toy makes a noise as it drops, or

b people laugh or shout at them for doing it.

Everybody likes to be noticed!

This is a natural part of what children do, and it is necessary to help their understanding of the world. However, if this habit becomes too firmly established it might be difficult for your child to move on to other things. So perhaps we should enjoy the throwing activity but enjoy other things the child does too and not single out throwing for too much attention.

Guidelines if your child becomes obsessed with throwing

1 You should introduce other activities for which she gets attention.

2 Always try to play down any angry reactions you may have to her throwing. An effective approach seems to be to anticipate and attempt to intercept every throw, by saying: 'Give it to me', and make sure that the object does get into your hand from hers. Then quickly say 'Good girl' or 'Thank you'.

3 Put a large tin beside her which makes a nice resounding 'ping' as she drops the toy into it.

4 A persistent thrower may need to have toys attached to her chair on elastic so that they come back to her.

5 Try to create a situation for your child in which throwing is appropriate and acceptable, for example ball games, velcro dart balls, target games, or throwing a small beanbag at a tin lid.

6   Try to give renewed satisfaction, by encouraging her on to the next stage, which involves exploring boxes, tins, bags, and other containers, to see what they contain. Your child will need help to find and explore what is in containers.

Exploring containers

Give your child boxes, tins, old handbags, a laundry basket and plastic containers. Add to these lots of odds and ends which can be put into them, such as toy bricks, hair rollers, other tins and boxes, things to squeak and all kinds of junk materials, safe to play with. Saucepans, wooden spoons, lids, old large cardboard boxes, scarves in which to wrap things and old hats all make good toys at this stage. Sighted children begin to be fascinated by what is inside all kinds of containers and go through this stage naturally. We may have to direct a multi-disabled visually impaired child more specifically.

a   Let your child shake a slinky spring in a tin and direct her hands into the tin.

b   Encourage your child to shake an open tin with a wooden brick in it and then coax her to put in a hand, to find the brick.

c   Let her delve into different varieties of bags (not Mum's handbag!).

d   Large cardboard boxes and laundry baskets are useful to climb in and out of.

e   Lentils, macaroni and rice, in different shaped containers, tempt a child to shake them about, to reach in and pick up a handful, to sprinkle elsewhere, even to smell and taste (be watchful), tip over herself, and possibly step on with bare feet. (Make sure she does not put them in her ear or nose!)

f   Old hats, shoeboxes, tins, and baskets can be put on her head, over her hands and arms, on her feet, as also can bracelets and chunky necklaces.

g   Your child may be moving about the floor more now and beginning to be interested in cupboards and drawers. Try to

leave a cupboard or a drawer that you do not mind her exploring, but watch that she doesn't trap her fingers when opening and closing the door or drawer. Most children go through a stage of tremendous activity, pulling out pans and lids from the kitchen cupboards.

h A first posting box might be a transparent plastic sweet jar, obtainable free from your local sweet shop. Make use of balls, clothes pegs, fir cones, and so on for posting. Once your child has the idea she will fill the jar herself because hopefully by this time she will be finding her way about the room, or even further afield, and will discover things on the way.

The jar is especially useful when a child has a small degree of sight because she can see the objects inside and watch the movements of her fingers.

i Encourage experimenting with all the containers and materials, putting small objects into large ones, shaking them about, trying in other containers, and so on.

Matching and fitting

Children begin to realise that some things do not fit when they try to put the wrong lid on a container. They are 'too big' or 'too small'. This adds a new, special understanding, and helps language.

Your child will need to be given the opportunity to experiment with all sorts of containers which have lids.

a   Let her climb into a very large old, suitcase and pull the lid down (remove locks and be on hand in case she is frightened by seeming to be shut in).

b   If you give her a cardboard box with a flap lid, perhaps she will experiment with the lid, opening and closing it, listening as it flaps back, or maybe reach inside, or put something inside and close the flap. The conventional type of music/jewellery box has a hinged lid, which is inviting to lift, especially if a child is not well motivated otherwise.

c   Cardboard boxes which have flap tops or drawers (for example household size matchboxes) or tins with easily worked hinged lids are useful learning tools, as are saucepans with lids to remove and replace.

Further developments in using hands

The sighted child

As sighted children begin to use their hands more, they develop more sophisticated skills leading to greater precision and strength.

Fingers and wrists Children begin to strengthen their hands as they use them more and more.

Using finger and thumb together Sighted children develop the skill of picking up things they see with thumb and finger, and become increasingly proficient at it, as hand-eye coordination improves.

Separating fingers Children learn to use their fingers one by one, for example on a keyboard, or putting on gloves.

Rotating the wrists There are many toys and activities that encourage twisting and turning movements, so strengthening a child's wrists.

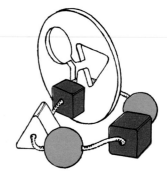

Gaining strength Children's hands gain strength through a range of activities, pulling and pushing toys for example.

The visually impaired child

You can begin to make things more complicated for your child to explore. 'Pick and mix' activities which involve your child in using:

- finger and thumb together
- fingers in separation
- fingers and wrists
- wrists in rotation
- squeezing, pulling and pushing

This will give your child strong hands through which to learn.

Partnership activities to encourage complex use of hands

a   For further development, try putting a hole or slit in the lids and boxes so that your child has to control her hand movements to a more specific degree in order to put things in. She will also discover that some things will not fit and will probably get upset about it, but encourage her to try other things.

b   Toyshops sell a wide range of shape sorter posting boxes. Start with easy ones which only have a few holes and shapes.

c   Many children find toys such as Pop-up Men (Galt) or a Pop-up Jungle/Farm (Boots/Early Learning Centre) enjoyable at this stage.

d Now is a good time to introduce toys such as brightly coloured rings of decreasing size stacked on a pole, or a wooden stacking clown.

Your child may need opportunities to become more supple, to strengthen flabby fingers, or to develop wrist rotation.

This is helped as your child begins to use her hands together in more and more refined ways.

All through these activities try to get your child to use two hands together in the way that they will need to later on when 'educational' activities are introduced such as rings on a stick, painting, crayoning, or modelling. This two-handed coordination will help towards self-care activities, such as dressing and undressing, fastening buttons and buckles, using cutlery and ultimately using equipment such as radios, cassette recorders, telephones, and so on.

Consider the finger movements needed for pulling a zip down, producing a tune on a piano or organ, pressing the start button on a radio, undoing buttons, telephone dialling, putting coins into a coin box or pressing keys on a computer keyboard. All of these encourage children to use and strengthen their fingers.

Exploring with hands

Visually impaired children find fewer opportunities for exploring unless people provide special ones.

a Let your child play with small beads **safely** strung on a cord.

b Put Smarties, pieces of chocolate buttons, or jelly sweets on a tray for her to pick up.

c Make knots at intervals along a cord for her to find.

d Children often enjoy handling the bobble ends of antennae on toys such as a 'Clatterpillar'.

e Encourage children to make a finger/thumb rubbing movement, under supervision, on pieces of wrapping film, biscuit papers, corrugated card, velvet, silk and ribbon.

f Let your child pick out shiny cake decorations from amongst pieces of pasta.

Separating fingers

a Play at putting plastic or wooden rings on your child's fingers, and let her put them on yours.

b Very large beads, round elastoplast tins, lengths of tubing, have holes in which children like to poke their fingers.

c The tops of biros are about the right size for fitting on the tops of fingers. Drumming fingers individually on a tin then makes a good noise. (Do not do this if she bites and mouths her toys.)

d Sew fancy buttons on the finger tips of gloves. Click together thumbs and fingers, or make them dance on the table.

e Treacle on fingers has to be licked from each individual one.

f Play with string. Wind it loosely around her fingers and thumbs.

g Encourage her to use fingers individually on a toy organ or piano.

h Several toys have push buttons, good for little fingers.

i Finger puppets are interesting for use with rhymes and action stories.

j Enjoy singing together and acting out finger rhymes, such as 'Incey wincey spider' and 'Peter pointer'.

Wrist rotation

a Make sure your child has plenty of toys with knobs which are easy to screw and which make clicking noises or music when the knobs are turned.

b Many used household items have unscrewing and screwing possibilities. One ribbed plastic cup rotated inside another provides a most interesting sound.

c The lids of empty plastic mineral water bottles can be screwed and unscrewed.

d Finding sweets or other things hidden inside screw top plastic bottles is fun for your child.

e In unscrewing empty face or hand cream jars, the lingering perfume, and possibly traces of the cream can be discovered.

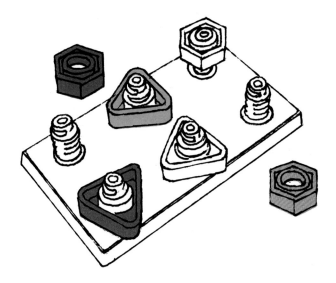

Useful materials for developing hand strength and different actions

Squeezing

a Squeakers.

b Empty plastic washing up liquid bottles from which a child can expel air and direct it onto her cheek or the palm of her hand. Used in the bath, she can squeeze out the water.

c Sponges during water play.

d Finger castanets.

e Plastic fruit storers or egg cartons produce interesting sounds when squeezed.

f Flour, oil and water dough.

g Blu-tack being very elastic, is super for pulling and squeezing.

h Wooden acrobat. A squeeze makes him turn over.

Pulling

a   A pop gun.

b   A pull-string talking toy.

c   A musical box with a string.

d   Blu-tack or elastic to pull out.

e   Pieces of velcro to pull apart.

f   An acrobat puppet.

g   Jumping Jack puppet.

h   Pull-string lights.

Pushing

a   Drawers or doors to close – mind fingers!

b   A humming top.

c   A pop gun.

d   Pianos and organs.

e   A doorbell.

f   A 'Pop-up' Jungle (Boots) or Farm (Early Learning Centre).

g   An electric switch.

h   A switch-on torch.

i   A truck to push along.

Chapter 3

The space beyond me

Children need a self-image so that they can relate to people and the world beyond them. Sighted children become aware of their bodies and what is beyond themselves because they can see. Visually impaired children discover their world through bodily movements.

What the world looks like when you are on your tummy

The world looks different when you are on your tummy, compared with being on your back, or moving your head to look around.

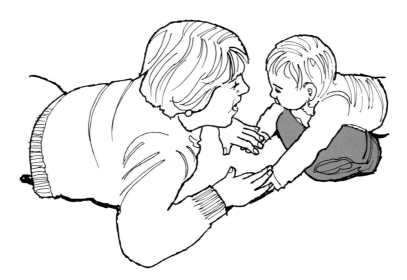

Here are some activities which involve a child being on his tummy. Your child may not like being on his tummy, or may only be happy to be like this for a short time. Don't insist. There are many positions for your child. Change the position, cuddle, make it fun and interesting for him. This will help your child to learn about the space beyond himself, and to use his body to explore the world beyond, for example by control of the head, hands, by sitting, crawling, or walking. Lying on his tummy gives your child a different experience of the world beyond him.

Partnership activities when your child is lying on his tummy

At first lift his shoulders by letting him rest with his chest over a folded blanket, rolled-up mat or pillow. It is important for your child to learn to lift his shoulders and chest whilst on his tummy.

a   Lie on the floor in front of him, face to face, and talk. Encourage him to put his hands flat on the floor, perhaps using vibration on the floor, or play games with his hands and your hands together.

b   Let him reach to touch your face or help him to do so.

Very important: Do not leave your child for so long on his tummy that he gets totally miserable. Change his position, cuddle him, talk to him, play games and so on, whilst he is still enjoying himself.

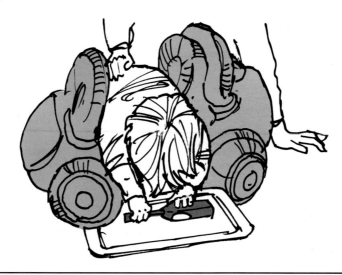

c Place him over a rolled up blanket or cot mattress or a peek-a-boo inflatable roller; put things in front of him which he can reach to touch or bang or which fascinate him visually, such as:

- a toy which tinkles and rights itself when knocked
- a bobbly musical box
- a tin or wooden tray containing a ball or large wooden beads to knock or roll about
- a pillow-case filled with paper to pat on to make scrunchy noises
- press-ping bell to pat
- crinkly papers and foil
- a 'slinky' spring
- a biscuit tin with polystyrene balls or cotton reels to knock so that they roll around
- a shallow box of pasta shapes or cornflakes to 'swish' at with his hands
- a toy organ
- a vibrator in a box or on the floor
- a bowl of bubbly water to 'dabble' hands in
- sponges in water to squeeze and squash
- corks in water to pat at so that they bob about
- ping pong balls to knock around on a metal tray. (Not for children who put things in their mouths!)
- suspend attractive or noise-making toys from a frame for your child to swipe at
- if he has sight, prop up a mirror, facing him
- fold up a survival blanket, put it in front of him. It shines and if he touches it, it makes 'scrunchy' noises.

Saving reactions

Sighted babies react to falling forwards by extending their arms to protect themselves. They right themselves as they fall to the side or forward when they begin to sit. These are known as 'saving reactions'.

Encourage these saving reactions as you play with your visually impaired child, as this will help him towards sitting and standing balance, good posture and mobility. Visually impaired children may need help in realising that the floor is a continuous surface.

Saving reactions when moving forwards

a   If your child is fairly small, use a squeaky, inflatable car as a support under the child's chest; roll him gently forwards and back so that the car squeaks. Next, if he is enjoying it, gradually tip him as you hold him firmly, long enough for him to touch first the floor in front with his palms, then behind with his feet. Support him very well.

b   If your child is fairly small, place him face downwards, over a peek-a-boo roller. Position yourself on the floor so that you are face to face with him. Call his name and rock him forwards towards you so that his open hands touch the floor and you touch noses with him. Then push him gently back on his knees, still supporting him.

c   Put a small vibrating device against a board or in a box. Place him on his tummy over a roll with his hands forward, touching the board or box.

d   Hold him firmly around the body or between your knees, with his back to you and arms up. Have a fun game with appropriate words, tilting him forwards towards the floor, so that his hands touch the floor before you lift him upright again. Keep him very well supported all the time so that he feels secure.

e   Whilst you sit with legs outstretched, lie him on his tummy over your legs, with face and arms forward. Hold his legs securely whilst you make more of a slope with yours. Allow him to slide down onto his palms.

f   Rock, swing, sway and bounce him in energetic fun – your child is learning to experience himself in all kinds of positions.

g   Lie him on his back over a very large beach ball. Hold his wrists and bring his hands to your face. His head will drop backwards slightly.

h   Put him on a springy mattress or trampoline and bounce it up and down, so that he has fun trying to right himself.

i   When another adult is available, take it in turns to squirm about like a snake while your child lies forward on your back, his hands dangling on your shoulders, steadied by your partner. In this way your child will experience the variations in tilting movements.

Developing head control

A sighted baby will make early attempts to raise or turn his head whilst propped up in a sitting position or lying on his tummy. He will be rewarded by seeing things which are attractive, and people who smile approvingly as they establish eye contact.

A visually impaired baby does not have such natural stimulation and needs help to gain head control. Many may not even want to be in a position other than lying on their backs. Often, visually impaired babies do not turn their heads towards a sound but 'still' to listen. This is a very good sign, but might not be noticed easily. When muscles are tense, or floppy, maintaining head control is hard. Here are some activities which help head control to develop.

a   When your child is sitting on your lap, in his chair, or is lying prone, stroke him and talk to him; then these positions will have enjoyable and interesting associations.

b   As he lies on the floor, lie beside him face to face. Rub noses, talk to him and kiss him, cuddle and caress him.

c When he is on his tummy or in a well-supported sitting position, blow gently or squeeze air from an empty plastic perfumed bottle on his hair. He may raise his head to feel the breeze.

d When he is lying on his back, tuck a folded cot blanket or small cushion under his lower neck and shoulders. This helps him to relax his shoulders and bring his arms forward. Hang visually attractive or sound producing objects on a frame above him to stimulate his interest.

e Lying him on his back with support as above, bend both his knees on to his chest or rest his legs on your shoulders, and lean over him. Take his hands separately, then together, so that his palms can feel your face and hair. Talk to him all the time.

f Place him, face forward, over a very large beach ball. Hold his hips while you move the ball gently backwards and forwards.

g Lie on your back on the floor and have him lying prone on top of you, face to face. Talk and sing to him.

h Lie the child (if he is small) on his tummy across your knee. Talk above his ear and reward any slight lift with a kiss and praise.

i Tickle him under the chin. Maybe he will lift his head. Praise him when he does so.

j Touch his head lightly with a balloon or feather duster. Encourage him verbally to lift his head.

k Place a handkerchief on his head so that he may try to get rid of it.

l If your child is small, lie him on a blanket. Get your partner to face you, while you both lift a side of the blanket for a few centimetres/inches alternately, so that the child turns very slightly to one side, then to the other

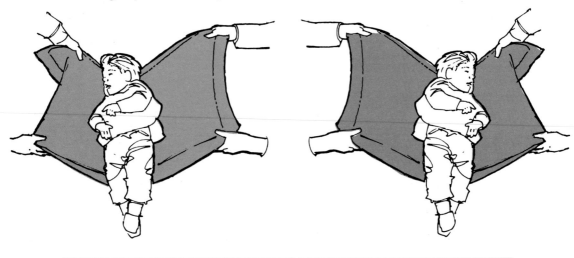

m When he is sitting supported, rest his head against the inflated inside of a wine box, or air cushion, or pillow case filled with scrunchy paper, so that he is encouraged to move the back of his head.

n Have him sit facing you on your lap with his head and shoulders well supported in your arms. Sing to him and make rocking movements. Be very sensitive to any efforts he may make towards initiating more rocking movements.

o When you know he has established some head control, kneel over him as he lies facing you on his back. Hold his hands and gently encourage him to lift and lower his head as you say 'up' or 'down'.

Learning to sit up

Children can see more when they sit, and they can link this with sounds they hear.

Sitting has advantages because in this position it is easier to hear which direction a sound comes from. Children with residual vision can see more, and it is easier for them to bring their hands towards objects and hold toys as they play with them. It is easier to learn where their toys are when they drop them.

Some children resist sitting because they are more secure if the whole body is in contact with a firm surface. Life is also easier lying down! Encourage your child to sit in a variety of places at different levels. Make it interesting, because it is boring to sit with nothing going on.

Partnership activities to encourage sitting

Support him sitting on your lap to talk against his cheek and sing to him. As soon as he has some degree of head control, prop him firmly in a corner of a settee, in a baby relax chair, or on the floor with his back to the settee surrounded by cushions.

a Talk to him face to face

b Talk against his cheek

c Sing to him and play with his hands, bringing them together.

When he has some degree of head control, sit on the floor with him, his back resting against your chest:

a   Cuddle him. Blow above his head. Talk into his ear. Encourage him verbally to raise his head.

b   Hold his hands and bring them forward into midline to rub together, or play 'pat-a-cake'.

c   Hold his arms and rock him from side to side so that his hands touch your legs alternately.

d   Sing 'see-saw' as you sway him from side to side. Help him to touch the floor at each side alternately. When he has gained confidence, let him sit on the slightly inflated inner bag of a wine carton to add an interesting 'wobble'.

e   Hold his arms and play a singing game which involves his leaning forward to touch the floor.

f   Whilst he is sitting, supported, put some 'scrunchy' paper on the floor in front and encourage him to lean forward onto his hands.

g   If you have found that he has some sight, however little, shine a torch onto a mirror or diffraction disc on the floor in front of him as he sits and encourage him to touch it with both hands.

Sit him in a chair which supports him well, preferably with strap or pommel to prevent him slipping down. (You may need advice from your physiotherapist.) Make sure there are interesting things to do or experience. For example:

a   A tray in front provides a base for putting toys or other materials on, for him to dabble his hands in.

b   Things which are visually attractive or make a sound when touched can be hung in front of him from a frame.

c   Facing him at his level, talk and sing to him.

d   At this stage, it may be appropriate to give him food and drink whilst he is in such a chair.

Sit him in a swing, well supported at the neck and trunk, if you know that it is necessary. Put his hands forward to grasp the rail, then gently rock him back and forth.

Once his back is stronger and head control is established, he will need a chair with some support at the back and sides, but not for his head. Ask your physiotherapist for advice.

a   Floor level wooden chairs give some support and allow floor level play. These can also be used in conjunction with a low table. On the other hand, a cardboard box can be used as a table when one side is cut away to allow room for his legs. A vibrating device on the box gives it a rather interesting sensation for his hands.

b   An old car tyre gives some support to the lumbar region, but still provides a possibility of playing with toys put on top of the tyre or of leaning over safely to touch things outside the ring of the tyre.

c   Once a child has some strength in his back, as well as head control, he may enjoy sitting inside a sturdy cardboard box. It will give him some support and balance whilst providing several opportunities for play. It has surfaces on which to tap and scratch. By piercing small holes in the box, toys can be suspended inside. **Safe** materials, textures, and objects with tactile and sound potential in the bottom of the box are good for exploration with hands or feet.

d   Now try sitting him facing you on your lap or between your legs and his hands held in yours. Play at swaying backwards and forwards, perhaps singing 'Row, row, row the boat'. Make sure he is lifting his head properly.

To achieve unsupported sitting, a child must be able to use his hands and arms to save himself from falling sideways, backwards and forwards. Go to the 'Saving reactions' section near the beginning of this chapter to find out how to help him learn to do this.

Beyond self

Sighted babies learn to explore the space beyond themselves, and use their bodies to do so. They are motivated to begin moving about the room by seeing things.

Visually impaired babies need help in realising that there is a world beyond themselves. They tend to be happy remaining on the spot to play and listen. Moving your child about and talking, describing what is happening and where they are, so that it is meaningful to the child helps him to realise that there are exciting corners to explore and things to find.

Activities to encourage awareness of the world beyond self

a   Change your child's position throughout the day. For example, place him on his tummy (perhaps over a roll or wedge) or just on the floor, or on his back with mobiles strung above him or propped into a sitting position in some way.

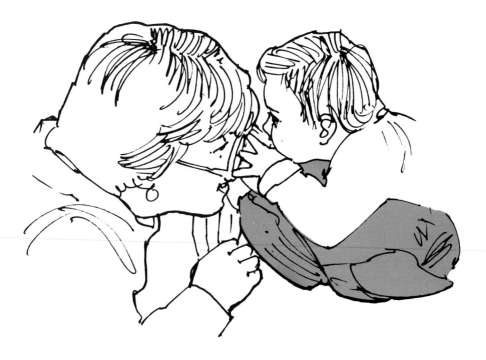

b   Place him in various parts of the room so that he gets to know each area of it.

c   Get accustomed to moving him from room to room as you work to help him to recognise each, by its smells and sounds.

d   When you are with another adult, lie him on a blanket, get hold of two corners each, and swing him gently.

e   Have fun with him bouncing, swaying, swinging and so on, so that he gets used to body movement. You will probably find he rather likes it. In our experience dads are good at having this sort of physically energetic play with their children. Visually impaired children sometimes enjoy the rough and tumble activities of other children in the family.

f   Roll him from one side to another. Ask your physiotherapist the best way to do this safely.

g   Encourage him to expect that, when he reaches out, he will find something interesting. Whether he is lying or sitting, put things close by for him to find.

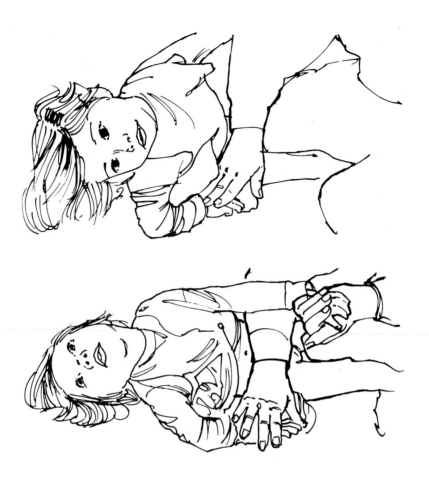

h   Play games which involve moving, or being moved, in some way towards someone else who is calling his name, and who gives him hugs and kisses when he arrives.

i   Encourage him to reach out to touch toys which have a sound.

j   Lie on your back on the floor and let him lie on top of you, face to face. Squirm about the floor with him.

k   Lie face down on the floor with him face down on your back, with his arms on your shoulders, so that he feels your body moving as you squirm around.

l   Make a point from time to time, of moving about the room with him, so that he encounters walls, doors, furniture, windows and so on. If he can take some part in the movement, that is good.

m   Think of the places non-disabled children get into when they are little, and let him experience similar places, for example under a coffee table or chair, behind a settee, over the top of a pouffe, beside a washing machine which is working, and so on.

n   Hold him firmly as he lies on his tummy for a minute or two on the bottom two or three stairs. He should then experience the contour and slope of the stairs on his body, and enjoy taking a little weight on his knees or feet.

o   Let him be on a mattress whilst other children are bouncing on it. (Supervise!)

Crawling

Sighted babies crawl spontaneously. They see something interesting and move towards it.

Visually impaired babies often do not crawl spontaneously. It can be very frightening in a large space. The baby must want to crawl, but may need help. If he enjoys being on his tummy, you can use his hands to reach out, raise his head, and help him to sit with balance. The following activities will encourage crawling.

Getting ready to crawl

A child is getting ready to crawl when he
- enjoys being on his tummy
- bears weight on his hands and knees, and rocks

- has sitting balance
- has saving reactions
- reaches beyond himself to get things
- can reach to find sound-making toys
- shows some interest in moving on the floor in some fashion
- has inner motivation
- has space and somewhere to go
- gets encouragement and praise appropriately.

Put your child in a play pen with toys and objects which make sounds hanging on the bars. Your child might be encouraged to reach out and crawl towards the sounds as they are not too far away.

Standing

When sighted children are propped up to stand, they can look at a stationary object and adjust their body in line with it. Walking increases the ability to get around and to find out 'what is beyond me.'

You need to make your visually impaired child feel safe about moving into unknown space. It is important to talk to your child as he moves, giving words to describe each activity. Be careful not to pass on your natural fears and anxiety for your child's safety in your words or tone of voice.

The following activities will encourage your child to explore 'what is beyond me':

a   When he is ready, encourage him to stand propped between your legs as you sit to play with him, or put his favourite toy on the settee for him to reach.

b   Put his favourite toys just beyond his reach and encourage him to stretch to get them, even if you have to help him. One child will reach towards the sound of a musical box, another to get a shiny toy.

c   A safe baby walker with a canvas seat might have some use for short periods at this point to encourage moving around on his feet. Long periods of use are not advisable because you are trying to develop his balance as well.

d Roll a very large brightly coloured and tinkling ball near him. Encourage his movements to get it. If he has no real independent movement, a low trolley or perhaps a walking frame may be helpful here. (Seek advice about safe and suitable walkers.)

e If he has no sight, play with him, rolling an electronic bleeping ball (RNIB). Encourage him to anticipate its arrival and reach or move to get it.

f When he is ready, encourage him to stand by furniture to play.

g Get him to move along a piece of the furniture a little. He may need the encouragement of a toy or a drink, or a sweet, or may just have to be shown that to move this way is an enjoyable experience.

h Move two pieces of furniture a little way apart so that he gains confidence in moving from one to the other.

i Develop his ability to pull up and let himself down by playing 'up and down' games, holding his hands, also 'Ring o' Roses' and so on.

j As you walk, let him walk on your feet, well supported.

k Erect some parallel bars by slotting and tying broom handles very securely into the backs of four firm chairs. The child then holds each bar to walk inside the narrow passageway formed.

l Some children benefit from swimming and leisure centres often organise 'water-baby' sessions when children can experience freedom of movement in a new way. Approved blow-up aids to floating may be helpful. Medical advice should be sought first, to ensure that it is appropriate and safe for your child to go swimming.

m When a child can walk with fairly light support, useful aids are:
- reins and harness with bells on. Visually impaired children often take a long time to develop from the stages

of being supported to free walking and reins help to give the feeling of independence.

- a **weighted** push baby-walker, or pram, can also provide an aid at this stage. (Seek advice about a safe walker.)
- a hoop. A child gets inside and holds onto the front while an adult holds the outside. You can pretend this is a game of 'riding a horse'.

n   Don't stop a visually impaired child from exploring stairs. He will learn best of all about stairs if he is allowed, under supervision, to crawl with his whole body outstretched on them. Walking up with a hand held, or holding a rail, comes later. He will probably want to crawl or slide down on his tummy to begin with, so help him to slide down gently, feet first.

Partnership activities to encourage movement

Playing 'in' and 'out' For this fun game, you need a large cardboard box or laundry basket. Play at climbing in, being pulled about and gently tipped out.

Playing 'underneath' and 'on top of' Show him how to wriggle underneath and bang on the underside of an old coffee table or climb on top of a pouffe and play at sliding off.

Playing 'through' Obtain a large cardboard box, open at each end.

a   Help your child put his head inside one end whilst you put your head in the other. Talk or shout to each other. Knock and scratch on the sides.

b   Gently help your child move his way through the box to the other end.

c   If your child finds great difficulty in moving at all, add interest inside the tunnel by making holes in the top to dangle ribbons with interesting things attached, or lining the inside walls with pieces of corduroy or other materials.

Playing at 'inside' For this you need a fireside rug or very large sheet of brown paper or small blanket. Play at rolling him over and over, starting at one end, so that gradually he is rolled up in the paper or blanket. Gently unroll it letting him roll over and over.

Playing at 'finding the edges'

a   Help him go round the walls of a room.

b   Use a fireside rug or an old mattress: have him stretch out wide to find the edges. Help him roll from one end to the other end and back again.

c   Play at 'There were ten in a bed' using a mattress. Roll him over or roll over beside him as he does so until he rolls off the end.

Playing at 'along' If you have a pine kitchen bench or a long plank of smooth shelving (without splinters), let him be face down, holding the edges, and help him to pull, push and slither from one end to the other.

Playing going 'up' and 'down'

a   Let him jump 'up' and 'down' on your lap or on the floor, well supported. This is fun.

b   If he is small and light, put him in a strong cardboard box and give him 'aeroplane rides', moving him around at shoulder height.

c   Let him jump on a trampoline, possibly holding his hands.

d   Play singing games with him, such as 'Jack in a Box' or 'Ring o' Roses' which involve jumping 'up' or falling 'down'.

e   Go to the swings and swing 'up' and 'down'.

f   Play at jumping up and falling down on an old mattress.

g   If he is light enough, let his dad lift him up to touch the ceiling.

h   Find a place where there is a suitable slide for him to slide down safely.

i   Help him to discover the pleasure of rolling **down** a grassy bank. (Supervise!)

Playing outside

a   If at all possible help him to discover low walls outside. Help him to climb on them and jump off. (Supervise!)

b   When out for a walk together, help your child be aware of and explore the post box, telephone box, lamp posts, gateways, bushes, trees and gratings.

c   Help him to become aware of different surfaces out of doors – tarmac, grass, leaves, twigs, pavement as well as carpet, lino, wood and tiles inside your home.

When your child is very much more active, the following activities may be helpful.

a Play games in which he has to stretch up high or wide, make himself small, or touch his toes.

b Let him lie on the carpet without shoes and see how far he can stretch his fingertips and toes.

c Get him to pretend to walk like a dog.

d Encourage him to walk on grass verges – one foot on the path, the other on the grass. Vary the game by jumping from grass to path and back again.

e Great fun can be had walking in and out of puddles, round the edges, or jumping in them in wellington boots! Interesting surfaces can be found for playing similar games, for example rocks and sand at the seaside.

f Play at walking backwards with him.

g Scatter some cushions or sheets of paper around the room, with small gaps between them. Get your child to climb or step from one to the other without touching the floor. Gaps can be widened for added interest as proficiency develops.

h Get him to climb from the inside of one rubber tyre to another and another.

i Find something to make strong, steady 'stepping stones' for your child to climb on, or walk from one to the other. (Later vary the heights.)

j Let your child have fun with a hoop, wriggling through it in different ways.

k Have him crawl or walk round the edge of a large rubber tyre.

l On outings, find fallen tree trunks over which your child can climb, pull himself up, crawl or walk.

m Introduce an obstacle course of furniture or objects which he has to negotiate by squirming through and climbing under, over, around, between, up, down, in, out and so on.

n A hanging rope, rope ladder, or scrambling net helps a child to appreciate his own body weight as well.

o Let him experience a see-saw or balancing board.

p Let him walk on stilts, strong cocoa tins on pieces of string, and pogo sticks. These are usually great fun and help the child to get a good balance.

q When he is ready (and he will not be so until he seems to have shown some preference for one hand) introduce games which focus his attention on his right. For instance, let him

---

wear a big glove (one of Mum's or Dad's) on his right hand. Emphasise that this is his right hand and that the other is his left. This glove might be worn for singing games like 'Hokey Cokey'.

r   'Simon Says' is a game which can be adapted for visually impaired children. Simon gives instructions, such as, 'Touch your toes', 'Pat your knees' 'Put your hand on your head' and 'Lift your leg'. If your child is wearing a glove on his right hand, you can make the instructions more specific, for example 'Put your right hand on your elbow, head, knee'. Later, add a progression – 'on your **left** foot, elbow, knee,' by slithering on his tummy, rolling, crawling, striding, walking toe to toe, or pushing his own wheelchair if he cannot walk. Try to combine listening with these activities so that your child begins to form some idea from the sound of a voice, for instance how far he has to go to reach the sound source.

s   An interesting trolley can be made easily at home from a length of smooth wood, four castors and castor blocks. Straps may be necessary for added support. Lying forward on the trolley can give a child a sense of freedom and independent mobility. In addition he can experience changes in sound and texture of ground surfaces, as well as gaining an opportunity to learn to steer and control a vehicle.

t   Think of activities with a scooter or roller skates as providing pleasurable sensations of movement.

u   If you are able to borrow an ASBAH (Spina Bifida) trolley from the local toy library, a child can sit and propel himself using the wheels to experiment with steering, as well as to enjoy a different perspective of the world.

v   In general, there are all sorts of singing games that are enjoyable, and which help a child build up his body awareness with rhythm, words and movements, and orientate himself in a larger space.

Exploring the environment

Sighted children develop a sense of distance through moving about in the space around them. It is difficult for a visually impaired child to get an idea of distance, and it is only by experience of movement that this will be learnt. For example, there will come a time when you can help your child to find distances from wall to wall in different ways. Hearing voices and discovering how far he has to go to reach the voice also helps.

Once children are mobile it is natural that they will experience objects such as furniture and buildings and what is outside – sounds and smells.

It is necessary to make sure that a visually impaired child gains a wide experience of what is beyond him. Help your child to gain confidence in moving beyond himself by describing and talking to him, during the experiences you share. In this way your child will begin to understand something about the space immediately around him.

Exploring the furniture Familiarity with the environment lessens fear. A visually impaired child needs help and encouragement to explore surroundings.

Exploring buildings Visually impaired children need someone to help them do this, so that they do not feel insecure and alone. They also need you to talk to them, to make sense of what they experience.

Exploring outside Because visually impaired children do not see what is outside, they need help in realising what is out there. Take your child out of doors and help him to feel where he is in space. Talk about where he is. Describe the immediate surroundings to him. Share the experience with your child, talking as you go.

The importance of people Other people are probably the most important thing in any child's life. Children learn through interacting with objects, places and events, but most of all they learn and develop through interacting with and sharing experiences with other people, especially those they love and who are important to them. This is the same for visually impaired children. Use these experiences to encourage your child to interact with you.

Exploring indoors: doing the washing

a   Put your child where he can feel and smell the dirty washing.

b   Let your child get up against the washing machine, or be on the floor nearby, to listen and smell, and feel the vibrations of the machine.

c   Place your child on his tummy on a wedge, dabbling his hands in a bowl of soapy washing, splashing, feeling, listening and smelling.

d   Let your child sit up in his chair amidst nearly dry washing on the line, listening to it flapping, feeling its movement against his face, and smelling its freshness.

e   Put your child on the floor to listen to the hissing of the steam and the 'plonk' of the iron – then let him feel the smoothness of newly ironed pyjamas, and enjoy their clean smell against his body.

Exploring buildings: learning about doors

a   Does your child know about doors? Position him by one. Let him listen to the sound as you open it towards him. Let him push it shut or help him to do so. Let him knock on the door, scratch on it, swing it backwards and forwards so that the draught wafts on him. Play with the handle. Listen to its sound. Use sentences such as 'Open the door', 'Close the door', 'Knock on the door', 'Listen to Tommy scratching at the door to be let in' and 'Turn the handle'. Supervise closely so that your child does not trap his fingers.

b   Position your child by the front door when the post or newspaper is about to arrive. Listen to the articles being pushed through and the letter-box snapping. Feel them as they come through. Say 'The postman is coming', 'The newspaper has come' and so on.

c   Let your child take some part in putting the milk bottles onto the step. Position him by the door when the milkman delivers. Listen to the footsteps up the path, the chink of the bottles and the receding footsteps. Let your child help open the door and collect the milk. Let him push the door shut. Say 'The milk has come' and so on.

Learning about windows

a   Sit with your child by an upstairs window so that he listens to traffic passing on the road outside, footsteps of somebody walking along, or dogs barking. Talk to him about them as they happen.

b   Position your child by a window when the window cleaner is outside it. Let him listen to the dabbing, rubbing and squeaking noises. Let him reach out to touch the window, rub and scratch at it, and slide a hand on it so that it squeaks.

c   Put him on or beside a piece of furniture which is interesting to tap or scratch at such as a corduroy, fabric or leather covered chair.

Learning about smells

a   Let him appreciate the different smells in the bathroom as he handles different objects, for example soap, talc and hand cream. Make special times for washing and bathing so that your child can get full sensory enjoyment.

b   Have him with you in the kitchen. When you are handling onions, carrots or potatoes and so on, give him samples of the vegetables to handle, taste and smell. Let him smell the food cooking.

c   Make a special event of opening various jars and tubes from cupboards. Let him smell the mustard, toothpaste, salad cream, shaving cream, jam, pickles or shampoo.

d   Position him by a cupboard. Let him be part of opening or closing it, making it click. (Supervise!)

Learning about sounds

a   Position him in a narrow hallway. Encourage clapping and vocalising to notice the difference in the sound there from that in an open space.

b   Change your child's position from a carpeted lounge, where sounds are softened, to a lino-tiled kitchen. (A ping pong ball dropped on the latter makes a fascinating sound as it bounces.) Let him be there when you sweep the floor with the broom, or mop it, if possible letting him be a small part of the action. Talk about what is happening.

c   Sit with him for a short while in the porch on a rainy day (well wrapped up!) so that he can fully appreciate the sounds of raindrops on the roof, the swishing as cars pass along the road and so on.

d   If you have a piano in the house, lean your child against it when someone is playing. Alternatively let him sit next to someone playing a guitar. Put him in a position for him to be able to push down piano keys or twang a guitar. Put him near someone practising any other musical instrument, for example, his brother or sister playing a recorder.

Exploring outside: ground surfaces

Even if your child is in a pram, buggy or wheelchair, exploring different ground surfaces can still be a rich, fun experience. Furthermore, if you dress your child in old clothes, and conditions are suitable, you may find opportunities to put him down at convenient spots to experience surfaces at first hand. Even if your child has very severe disabilities, it may be possible to give him the chance just the same. If you have ensured conditions are right, and are there to support and supervise him, he will not come to any harm and may enjoy the change.

a   A wood pathway covered in twigs and leaves makes crunchy and snappy sounds as you walk or push wheels over it. Its surface is interesting to roll on and to smell too.

b   Gravel has good sound appeal and also has a distinctive sound and feel.

c   Tarmac and flagstones make their own sounds when stepped on, and flagstones may give a regular bumping sensation when wheeled over. Tarmac gives a smoother ride.

d   Tall grass or sand provide distinctive touch and smell sensations and contrast with other surfaces.

e   Nearly all young children enjoy splashing in puddles in their wellington boots. If your child is small enough to support well, can you find some way he might experience this too in some measure?

f   When you have mown the lawn (provided he is not a hay fever sufferer) sit him on it and let him smell and handle the new-mown grass. Take him for a walk down a country lane after rain, or when sweet-smelling bushes are flowering.

Activities for the park

a   Sit with him listening to the other children talking, laughing, shouting, running and so on.

b   If at all possible, let him experience a swing or seesaw, with its special movements, squeaks and rhythms.

c   Draw attention to bird-song, barking dogs, the wind blowing and so on.

In the high street

a   Push him along a busy pavement in his buggy when cars, buses and bicycles are passing. Listen to engine sounds, hoots, brakes, bicycle bells and also to footsteps.

b   If you walk close to a wall, you will notice the sounds differ from those heard in open spaces.

c   Find a bridge to walk underneath. If your child can vocalise, he may enjoy calling out to enjoy the echo.

d   Take him for a walk near to roadworks. He will experience the various sounds and also the smell of tarmac. Be careful not to startle him.

Shopping

a   When you have time, make the most of shopping expeditions. If your child does not vocalise and he is unable to be in eye contact with people, you may find no-one talks to him because they need to be encouraged and convinced that he will actually like it.

b   When you go into a baker's shop or to the bakery counter at the supermarket to get bread, occasionally buy a small roll. Help your child, there and then, to break it open to smell and taste it.

c   Take your child into the fish and chip shop. Give him a chip in his hand in the shop so that he can smell and taste what you have bought there. (Make sure that the chip is cool enough to touch.)

d   You can repeat these experiences in other shops such as the florist, newsagent, shoe shop, delicatessen, greengrocer's or fruit and vegetable section at your supermarket.

Chapter 4

Eating and drinking

General hints on feeding for all children

Ensuring that their child is well nourished is important to all parents. The child's growth and general well-being is tangible evidence of their love and care.

Physically, learning to eat requires a child to be capable of:
- maintaining an upright sitting position
- controlling her arms in a range of movements
- grasping a spoon (or knife and fork) and controlling eating utensils with strong dextrous fingers
- rotating wrists in order to control the spoon scooping food, lifting the spoon to her mouth, keeping the bowl steady so that the food remains on the spoon, turning her wrist to ensure that the food goes into her mouth, and then rotating her wrist to replace the spoon on the plate or dish.
- Once the food is in her mouth, your child needs to keep it there, so lip closure is necessary and the child needs to be able to chew and swallow.

Therefore a child needs body balance, security of position, good head control, purposeful hands and an ability to associate control of the spoon with the necessary work of lips, teeth, tongue and jaw. She needs, too, experience of various textures and flavours of food. Some of these stages require certain physical maturity.

Socially, a child needs to interact with you and with other members of the family in this important, shared, family experience – namely, every meal time. It is an advantage for her to acquire good eating habits, pleasant table manners such as neatness and speed, and to adapt easily to eating out in a variety of different settings.

The emotional aspect of eating involves a child's attitude to food generally, likes and dislikes, her enjoyment or non-enjoyment of food, the ability to express her feelings about the food and sharing with others. Children will need to learn to associate certain foods with their respective textures, smells and flavours, so that they begin to discriminate mentally, to communicate likes and dislikes, and to remember which food was associated with which flavour, smell or texture. Your child will want more of something sometimes!

Learning to feed herself is a major step forward for every child. Visual impairment in itself, need not affect eating habits, yet at times it appears to do so, for a variety of reasons. How often the term 'finicky eater' is applied to a child with a visual impairment! How does learning to eat affect a child emotionally, socially, physically and mentally?

Learning to feed yourself is not a simple affair for any child. Why is it that some children seem to develop good eating habits easily while others do not? These are some of the features that promote good eating habits:
- close, early mother/child contact
- an adequate 'system', that is the child has no physical impairment
- the parent is generally calm and relaxed at meal times
- advantage has been taken of the child's natural urges when they occur for example the desire to bite, chew, hold the bottle or spoon herself
- new flavours and textures of food have been introduced gradually
- encouragement has been given to early finger feeding and its 'messy' aftermath, in a quiet, unhurried atmosphere with a parent who is not fussed
- the parent is not concerned if a child shows no inclination to clear the plate at each meal. He or she knows the child would not voluntarily starve herself
- the child will have been weaned as more and more solid foods have been introduced to the diet.

Visually impaired children

In thinking about the feeding problems of multi-disabled children, there are few who would fit the above descriptions. So, what is the result?

Many multi-disabled children may have been premature or 'small for dates' babies, or there may have been difficulties at birth, which resulted in the child being placed in a special nursing unit. The very early mother/child contact may be impaired.

Few multi-disabled children have a normal 'system'. Some children have an impairment that affects sucking and swallowing, biting and chewing; others have an impairment which affects the muscle-tone which helps a child to maintain head and body control with sitting balance, and assists controlled hand-eye and hand-mouth coordination. There are some children who may never chew or bite properly because of inadequate muscle control, poor coordination or severe developmental delay.

The mother of a multi-disabled child cannot feel calm and relaxed at meal times if she is anxious that her child is not getting sufficient nourishment or that she is not reaching 'normal developmental milestones' at the time she should. If she is an experienced mother, she cannot help but compare her child's progress with that of her other children, or with that of her neighbour's son or daughter.

This mother may well have attempted to establish a feeding routine but with little success because her child hates food, or shows only brief interest in meals. It may be that every meal time becomes an ordeal for both mother and child because the physical disabilities make feeding a long drawn-out process, or the child screams constantly or shows no attempt to learn how to feed herself.

Any attempt on the mother's part to allow the child to make a mess at meal times may well result in friction with other members of the family.

These are problems faced by the parents or teachers of multi-disabled visually impaired children, many of whom perhaps, may not achieve independent eating and drinking skills for many years.

Encouraging children to eat

Below are helpful hints for encouraging children who are reluctant to eat:

a Try to follow as normal a pattern as possible. A very young child should be held when being bottle fed and not propped up in the corner of a chair or settee, and she should never be left alone with a bottle in her mouth.

b If your child has poor muscle tone and is rather floppy, or is very stiff, it may be helpful to place her on your lap so that her head is supported in an upright position in the crook of your arm and her bottom rests between your legs, so that her knees bend over one of your legs.

c Once a child has good head control and sits with support, place her in a high chair (or its equivalent), ensuring that her feet are either comfortably supported by a foot rest or flat on the floor. It is important to provide a tray or table which is the correct height for the child when sitting, so that good sitting posture is encouraged. This will help her sitting balance both when supported and unsupported.

d It may be that your child still experiences difficulty in chewing food at this stage. Sit beside her with one of your arms around her so that her head is upright in the crook of your arm. You can then keep the child's head forward and resist any tendency for her to throw herself backwards. Food on the spoon may then be placed in the child's mouth with your other hand, whilst the first and second fingers and thumb of the supporting hand are spread to close the child's mouth and help her jaw to move in a chewing action.

e The spoon can be used for placing soft solids into a child's mouth after previously massaging her gums. Mothercare and Boots have produced sets of spoons which seem to be a useful size for most children. They are tough and can be boiled or sterilised.

These spoons can be used to give the child soft solids. Later she can be encouraged to learn to chew and bite by having fingers of bread, perhaps flavoured with jam, honey or marmite, put into the corner of her mouth.

f Some children may scream between spoonfuls. Screaming causes a greater intake of air, which may cause colic, which then results in more screaming. However, screaming is not always triggered off in this way. Try to observe your child carefully and adjust the timing between spoonfuls to satisfy her natural pace. The speed of eating will vary depending on how hungry she feels, how fond she is of that particular food, and whether it requires any chewing.

g Try to encourage her to bite and crunch a 'finger' of rusk, toast or biscuit, popped into the side of her mouth. If this is not successful, a piece of melon or pear may be used instead. Pear, or other soft juicy fruit, placed between a child's gums and teeth will encourage tongue movements, and breaks down easily for swallowing. Introducing more solid foods needs close supervision, while your child is learning to chew different textures.

h Finger feeding is a messy but essential part of a child's progress. Allow her to dabble her hands in her dish to feel the texture and consistency of the various foods, to learn to taste from her fingers and pick up slippery lumps. Cut up drier foods like sausage, chips, apple and so on, supervising her chewing closely. Help her hold rusks, bread, cake or biscuits in her hand, and keep holding after she has taken a bite. Introduce various flavours to encourage this.

i   When you are spoon-feeding a child you may find she reaches out to hold the spoon herself. This should be encouraged. Give her a spoon to hold whilst you put a spoonful of food into her mouth. Holding a spoon in this way helps her to 'make friends' with this tool and she will be learning something about its weight, size and shape as she handles it. It may be some time before your child will accept, hold and control the spoon and show more positive signs of wishing to feed herself.

Because of the possible link between chewing and speech, it is worthwhile persisting with this, however long it takes. It may help to get assistance from a speech and language therapist in establishing chewing. Feeding, whether by finger or spoon, is a very messy business for some considerable time, but independence in feeding skills gives a child so much pleasure and ultimately lessens the burden on mother and teacher, so try to persevere with this. Cover the floor with a large plastic sheet or lots of newspapers, cover your child (and yourself) well, or alternatively, dress her in easily washed clothes.

Learning to use a spoon

Let your child practise loading a spoon and bringing it to her mouth to encourage grip and wrist rotation. Give her food which sticks well to the spoon such as mashed potato.

She can also practise 'loading' by scooping sand onto a spade, soil onto a trowel, or catching floating corks, drinks cartons or small plastic ducks in a strainer in the bath!

A large spoon handle is easier to hold, so place a bicycle grip, foam rubber tubing, therapeutic putty or even 'Blu-tack', or splice a length of wood such as a piece of a broom handle onto the spoon to build up the handle, to enable your child to grip and control the spoon better.

Training a child to use a spoon by herself is a slow process and success often depends on taking advantage of signs which indicate that a child is sufficiently interested in food (or the spoon!) to want to 'have a go' herself.

A sustained hand grip is a necessary skill if a child is to succeed in manipulating a spoon to feed herself independently.

Use a hard plastic or metal spoon small enough to go into small mouths. Try to ensure that the food is in a bowl with straight sides or sides which slope inwards rather than outwards. This makes it easier for a child to scoop the food towards herself and upwards. Teach her to scoop from the centre out to the sides rather than from the sides inwards.

When being spoon-fed, if a child shows interest and tries to hold the spoon herself, it is advisable to give her a spoon while you pop another with food on it into her mouth. Feeding should give pleasure to both adult and child – it is a good time for socialising – and it is enjoyment of food and the 'togetherness' of the occasion which motivates the child to want to feed herself.

Activities to encourage your child to use a spoon

a   Ensure your child is comfortably seated in a chair with her back supported at the base of the spine and her feet on a footrest or flat on the floor (ready for eating her meal). It may be necessary to provide her with a non-slip mat or suction pad under her bowl on the tray or table to prevent the bowl from slipping. She is now ready to learn the steps leading to independent feeding.

b   Sit behind her, but slightly to one side, depending on which appears to be her preferred hand. Encourage her to pick up the spoon. Place your hand over hers and gently guide her spoon down into the dish and up towards the side of it. (A vertical-sided dish is best.)

c   Help the child to take the loaded spoon up towards her mouth. Let her put the spoon into her mouth.

d As she becomes more proficient in this action, gradually move your hand back towards her elbow, giving very slight support there until your child manages the action of raising a full spoon independently to her mouth.

e With this achievement, encourage her to fill the spoon herself more frequently. At this stage a child may want to use her other hand to push her food onto the spoon. She may spill a lot as she lifts the spoon. Do not worry about the mess or what seems to you to be a 'bad' habit. For a visually impaired child it is a very necessary stage of learning to feed herself.

Because she often loses quite a bit of food in raising the loaded spoon to her mouth, the child may become discouraged and need more persuasion and coaxing to hold her spoon. At this stage it is wise to intersperse some of her actions with a spoonful of food from your spoon. Encourage her to keep one hand on her bowl while she scoops the food. Your hand over her hand is a useful technique at this stage. Remind her from time to time to 'keep your chin up.'

First of all, let your child do the last step of the activity on her own, then the last two steps. Although you have to help with all the steps initially, and then all but one, and so on, she **finishes** the activity herself. Thus she is left with a feeling of success, and your praise and encouragement will reward her, so that she will want to continue doing more and more for herself until she has mastered the skill completely.

Encouragement and praise, plus lots of patience and good humour are the keynotes of successful training for every child, whatever the aspect of everyday life.

When spoon-feeding is very well-established and a child has had some experience of 'spearing' pieces of food with a fork, then the natural progression from spoon, to spoon and fork can take place. Learning to use a knife will follow but not until the child has had experience of using it on other tasks such as cutting plasticine or dough, spreading soft margarine or butter or jam on bread, cutting a bread slice into small cubes and so on.

While your child is learning to feed herself, she will be learning other concepts too, because you can talk to her about her **big** bowl (or it could be **red** or **round**); a **big** or **small** spoon; **another** mouthful; delicious **flavours/smell** as you name the vegetables, meat and so on. Her language and comprehension skills are being extended – another reason again for patience and persistence in teaching your child to feed herself.

Drinking

All children

As with eating, a child will need to be in a static sitting position, either on your lap with her back against your body, or in a high chair. A secure, comfortable sitting position is essential, whether she is at the stage of drinking from a bottle, a beaker with a spout, or an ordinary two-handled cup.

Early difficulties with drinking for children with impaired vision

Some children find it difficult to close their lips around the teat. This is essential for an efficient sucking action, and for the later development of drinking and chewing.

Encouraging your child to drink

When you are bottle feeding your child encourage her to place both hands on the bottle as you hold it. Put your hands over hers to keep them there. As she becomes proficient and begins to explore the bottle, encourage her to turn it around the right way and to hold it at a suitable angle while her head is supported. Do not allow her to arch her body and throw her head back while she drinks from the bottle.

Learning to use a cup

When transferring from a bottle to a cup, a two-handled cup is preferable to a beaker with a spout as it encourages a drinking rather than sucking action. Put a reasonable amount of liquid in the cup at a time, so that the cup does not have to be tipped up too far before the child gets some of the drink. However, the cup should not be so full that it is too heavy to hold. If it is too full the child is likely to choke on the first mouthful or get drenched. These are two very unpleasant experiences, and may well frighten and discourage the baby from wanting to learn to drink from a cup.

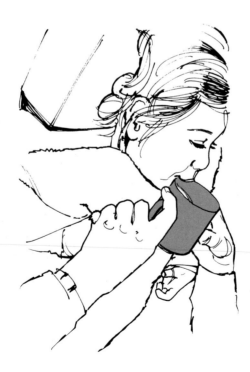

Put the cup between the child's lips so that the cup keeps the tip of the child's tongue down, thus overcoming 'tongue thrust'. If she tends to keep her tongue outside the cup her lips will not form a seal on the cup. She needs help to develop her lip muscles so that she is able to form a seal on the cup (and for chewing). Supervise very closely!

Partnership activities to encourage drinking

a Lightly tap her lips before she has a drink.

b Encourage her to blow a toy horn, flute or whistle.

c Encourage her to blow bubbles in the bath or to blow feathers or balloons across a table or into the air off her hand.

d Do not keep the cup (or beaker) in her mouth for long periods, otherwise the child will find difficulty in breathing. Double handled plastic cups are available from Boots and Mothercare.

e Put both her hands around the handles but encourage your child to keep her thumbs up the sides of her cup. At first, place your hands over hers on the handles of the cup with your thumbs up the sides. This grip should encourage a good head position. **Her head should be tilted forward, not back while she drinks.**

f If **the child** learns to control the process, she will find it easier to stop and breathe whenever she wants. Some children will still need help with drinking for a long time.

i After she has become accustomed to her cup, remember to introduce different flavours of drinks and to vary the temperature of the liquids – cold orange, cold milk or banana or strawberry milkshakes, **warm** chocolate, tea or coffee, Horlicks, Bournvita, Bovril and so on.

j When the child is able to hold objects with both hands, gradually remove the support of your hands. It may be necessary to help her tip the cup by putting your fingers lightly on its bottom. You will eventually be able to stop doing this.

k Encourage your child to hold the cup by herself.

l When she is able to pick up things with both hands, either hold the cup in front of the child so that she can reach for it, or put it down on the table before her with suitable comment.

m When your child has had enough, encourage her to 'give to Mum' (or her teacher) and try to prevent her developing the habit of dropping or throwing the cup.

n Encourage your child (with suitable praise) to 'put the cup on the table'.

Chapter 5

Washing, toilet training, sleeping and dressing

Becoming independent is one of the most important things in life. It means being organised, taking responsibility, actively doing and being interested in things. Sometimes we need help, sometimes we can get on with things by ourselves.

Washing, toileting, sleeping and dressing punctuate the routine of all children. Learning these self-care skills can make a tremendous difference to a child's independence and self-esteem. However, it also has to be acknowledged that if children have behavioural difficulties, these regular events can turn into a battle of wills. This chapter explores ways of making washing, toileting, dressing and bedtime as relaxed as possible, and discusses ways of encouraging appropriate behaviour.

Washing

Washing and bathing provide rich opportunities for playing with water and learning about its properties. Washing offers a chance to draw your child's attention to his own body.

Many children dislike having their hair washed. By talking, playing, joking and singing with your child while bathing, washing, cleaning teeth, you will be both reassuring and making it easier for him to learn from the experience.

Toilet training

This stage of a child's development is of major concern to parents of non-disabled and disabled children alike. Many parents proudly announce that a child is 'dry' or 'clean' at an early age only to find that, at a later date, their child appears to regress. There can often be a breakdown in the toilet-training, a child may wet the bed or withhold faeces or urine. Scolding and punishment do not help; in

fact, showing anger or disappointment at a child's behaviour just aggravates the situation.

To be successful in potty training, there are several points which should be considered:

a   **Maturity** of a child's central nervous system. A child will not be able to control bladder and bowel movements until the muscles controlling these organs are sufficiently developed to do their intended work.

b   A child will not be able to sit alone on his potty, or on a toilet seat until he has head control and body balance and can sit with his knees bent and apart, with his feet flat on the floor. If a child is physically disabled or totally without sight, he needs to be able to hold on to a supporting rod or frame in front of him.

c   Unless a child is capable of eating and drinking sufficient quantities of food, then there will be nothing to stimulate the bladder and bowel reactions. Your child should have a varied diet so that his bladder and bowels are working regularly.

d   Bowel control is achieved before bladder control.

e   Boys can take longer to train than girls.

f A child will usually be toilet trained during the day-time before night-time success is achieved.

g It really helps if you can maintain a relaxed attitude to toilet training. If you worry constantly, your tension will often be communicated to your child. 'Nagging' and angry reprimands achieve little except frayed nerves for you, and a stubborn reluctance to cooperate on the part of the child, who may not, in fact, understand what is expected of him.

h Are you ready to tackle this stage? Have you thought about what you will do when you are out? Is there someone who can help maintain the routine when you are not about?

All children

It is normal development for a non-disabled child to become truly 'clean' or 'dry' any time between the ages of two and four years.

Visually impaired children

It is equally 'normal' for a disabled child to acquire this skill at age four years or later. Much will depend upon the rapidity of maturation of his central nervous system, as well as other factors.

There are many points to remember when planning and establishing a toilet training routine.

If you note the frequency and/or time of the child's bladder and bowel movements you may see a pattern emerging, for example that your child may wet or dirty his nappy at fairly regular intervals through the day. This may be an indication of 'readiness' for a more formal or structured period of 'training', but there is no guarantee that this will be so with every child. All you can do is hope to succeed. If a trial period of training fails, then your child is not yet ready, and it is more sensible to postpone the training for a short time and try again later. Similarly if your child is unwell, it is wise to stop for a little while.

If a child shows signs of discomfort in his wet nappy, or when he has dirtied it, then regard this as a sign of readiness; take advantage of it and try to start some toilet training.

Toilet training activities

Ideally, toilet training should be done in the bathroom from as early as possible, so that your child connects going to the toilet with the bathroom. This is particularly important if a visually impaired child has additional disabilities. Of course, it is not always possible or convenient in a normal household and toilet training may be started in the kitchen or living room. There is no harm in this, provided that this situation does not continue past the time when your child is old and confident enough and capable of indicating that he wishes to use the potty.

Remember that when a child is happy to use a trainer seat on an adult-sized toilet, he will require support beneath his feet and perhaps a hand-rail, as we mentioned earlier. Remember, too, to ensure that every little response to the training is rewarded by lavish praise and encouragement.

Later stages in toilet training

From an early age, the establishment of a routine is **essential**. The following example of a routine is based on practices which have been used successfully by children in RNIB nursery schools over a period of several years.

For this, try to ensure that:

- your child has eaten or drunk sufficient quantities of food and liquid of the right kind so that his bladder and bowel muscles get the appropriate 'signal' to function. Physical exercise is important too, ensuring that his body functions are as normal as possible.
- the height and size of the potty, potty chair, or toilet seat is neither too high nor too low, nor too small, and see that your child's feet are touching the floor or supported by a box or platform, if necessary.
- check also that your child's knees do not touch his chin – if this happens the pressure movements for bowel action will be incorrect.

- a small child should not be left alone to sit on the potty. Verbal reassurance from an adult is important if he is to become confident in his training.

- a visually impaired child may feel more relaxed if he sits on his potty in a corner of the room where he is able to touch the walls on either side of him.

- a child will be more comfortable and relaxed if he is able to sit on a **warm** potty. It is a very frightening experience for a young child who does not see very well when he is put on a cold surface.

- a child may feel happier if the potty is put into a cardboard carton fitted with a bar across the end onto which the child can hold.

- for a child who has physical disabilities, a support frame which he can grasp to stabilise his balance may be necessary; this can be made at home, or perhaps, borrowed from your social services department.

- wet nappies, pants and sheets should be removed quietly and calmly without fuss or adverse comment.

- it is helpful if the child's mother (or familiar adult) is happy and relaxed, and willing to stay that way, for perhaps ten minutes at a time at frequent intervals throughout the day.

- most important of all, try to ensure that for every little response or effort made by the child, he is rewarded with lavish praise and encouragement.

- the potty or toilet must be regarded by your child as a 'friendly object' and not a 'threatening monster'. Remember that a relaxed, comfortable child will respond more quickly.

More toilet training activities

After indicating that he wants to go to the toilet, a child should be helped as follows:

a   Guide his hands to remove his pants.

b   Help him to sit comfortably or stand steadily so that he can 'perform'.

c   Help him to wipe his own bottom if this is necessary.

d   Encourage him to replace (pull on) pants, or to put the wet clothes into the bin and fetch clean, dry ones from a cupboard or drawer.

e   Show him how to push the handle, press the knob or pull the chain to flush the toilet.

f   Help him to wash his hands with soap immediately and to dry them carefully.

Ensure that the toilet paper is within easy reach and is always to be found in the same place.

Because of his interest in sounds, a child may wish to stand still to **listen** to the water flowing into the toilet pan and **feel** the water gushing from beneath the rim. He may wish to listen to the cistern filling up again, therefore be sure to be patient and allow time for these experiences – they are part of his education, and opportunities arise for extending his vocabulary, and explanations of cause and effect in emptying/filling cisterns, and so on.

Ideas for potties

A commode chair or a manufactured, plastic, moulded potty chair with arms may be necessary for an older, very disabled child.

One useful chair, complete with potty, is the Baby Relax Toilette. This is a miniature toilet, with seat and lid. When lifted the lid becomes the back of the chair.

A musical potty is sometimes helpful in toilet training – when urine reaches the base of the potty, a musical sound is produced.

Sleeping

Remember that bedtime is one of the most challenging times of the day for any parent. About one quarter of children are difficult to settle and do not sleep through the night until they are three years old, and sometimes older.

Sleep comes more easily to a child when there is a familiar and established pattern. To ensure that children feel relaxed, it is a good idea to provide some 'quiet' fun. Bath time is often a good time for this. A calm period should follow. Songs, rhymes, stories and cuddles or other close physical contact may be appropriate.

For example:
- a warm bath with bubble bath or bath oil and toys
- a bedtime story or story tapes
- playing a musical mobile
- singing or listening to songs with parents or brothers and sisters
- warm bed and pyjamas
- a favourite toy

There should be a familiar 'settling down' routine with any child. Bedtime can often be the time when problems surface more than at other times of the day. The parent is tired as well as the child.

All children need limits and boundaries to be set. Having no boundaries is in fact very frightening for children. Once your child is settled you can look forward to putting your feet up.

Behavioural difficulties

There is a temptation to feel you are being hard on a visually impaired child if he has to be managed firmly, but he needs that security just as much as a sighted child. Praise for effort and positive opportunities for success will best encourage good fun.

Some children, however, develop habits and/or behaviour difficulties which are not easy to manage. Although this may occur at any time of the day, bedtime is the time when these often seem worst for a parent. It is hoped that the following ideas may provide some clues about what to do, but bear in mind that there are no easy answers. Every child is unique: try out these suggestions to find out which works best for you and your child.

Head banging

Head banging is very distressing to watch. Head banging may be associated with one of the following:

Pain If a child persists and cannot be comforted or distracted, take him to the doctor to see if he has anything specifically wrong with him which is causing him pain. Your doctor may refer him to a specialist for electrical tests and scans to find out if he has any unusual brain rhythms, for which medication may be prescribed.

Pleasure/frustration If he seems to be doing it for pleasure or as a means of coping with frustration, you should try to anticipate occasions when he is most likely to indulge in head banging and distract him by offering an alternative pleasurable activity.

Attention seeking If you have established that a child's behaviour is not a reaction to pain, be careful not to reinforce it by scolding (which, strangely enough, may be pleasurable to him) or giving physical attention.

Tension Intense physical activity may be for some an alternative means of reducing tension.

Screaming

All children scream at some time or other. A child may use screaming to demand attention. He soon learns that you do not like it and uses it to get you to give in to demands that you would consider unreasonable, and cannot and should not meet, just so that he will shut up. Signs of this sort of screaming might be:

- he may give up screaming for a few seconds, as if listening to see what effect he is having.
- he may be easily distracted by something else which is interesting.

Is your visually impaired child screaming because he is frightened? Loud noises, new routines, being left alone without vocal reassurance, are all situations in which a child with impaired vision may be very apprehensive. Usually this reaction dwindles as familiarity with noise sources, new materials and new routines is built up over a period.

If your child screams all through the night, perpetually, it is essential that you consult a paediatrician, as the family cannot cope without sleep for any length of time. The paediatrician (child specialist) may be able to offer help. If you do not have regular advice from a paediatrician or have never seen one, ask your family doctor to help you get an appointment.

Screaming may be caused by colic. However, screaming causes a child to take in a larger intake of air, which makes a colicky pain more severe. It is a vicious circle.

It seems that some children are upset at certain times of the day. It could, of course, be for reasons previously mentioned such as hunger, colic or medication. On the other hand, some children take a long time to wake up fully in the morning, and dislike being 'messed about with,' while others who are cooperative and energetic in the morning, scream if approached later in the day. If your child is one of these you need to take advantage of his good times and during his disturbed periods, let him be in a quiet, calm, secure atmosphere, perhaps with someone he knows well, talking or singing to him. However, you may find your child responds in quite a different way.

Misunderstandings may arise because of a child's lack of language and life experience in realising that similar words can be used in widely differing situations. Take Alex, for example when he was out in the local shopping centre. He reached some stairs and was told, 'Go up the stairs, Alex'. He started to scream, to refuse to move and to say, 'Go up the stairs to bed, Alex'. When told 'No, not to bed', he went happily up without further fuss. Until then, 'stairs' had only been associated with bedtime. This anecdote emphasises our need to enrich a child's experiences of language in everyday life. We must be more receptive to what he is really trying to say and not make quick assumptions about bad behaviour.

Unusually over-active children

These children are difficult to contain at home, particularly where there are other small children to attend to, or there is a strong emphasis on tidiness, or rooms are small and there are many potentially dangerous objects about. Over-active children are easier to handle in the space of a school, but even then they can create many disturbances.

Over-active children have difficulty in attending to one thing at a time, and their attention is continually being attracted to other activities. The classic answer to their problem is to cut down the amount of stimulation available at any one time and to minimise other disturbing distractions. It works to a degree but is rarely the complete answer. A consistent routine and firm handling by one familiar person with a high degree of tolerance helps.

Recent research has shown that a few over-active children are allergic to certain foods and respond well to special diets. Discuss this possibility with your family doctor.

'Remote' children

There are some children who seem to be content in their own world. They wander around without seeking attention from anyone. They may crouch in a corner, assume an odd attitude or spin around on the spot. They may have a favourite object from which they don't want to be parted, or carry out strange mannerisms or feats of skill. They are withdrawn from normal emotional contact with people, which further disturbs their personality development and intellectual function. If you are concerned about your child's behaviour talk to your family doctor who can refer you to specialist help.

Partnership activities for children with behavioural difficulties

a   Try to discover a pattern. Does your child scream at certain times or in particular circumstances? Is he in pain? Is he a poor feeder, suffering from hunger or colic? If that is the case, medication or improving his feeding habits may be the appropriate approach.

Anticipation of all kinds of situations where this sort of screaming might occur is helpful, so that, as soon as there are any signs that he is going to start, sidetrack him by singing, tickling, energetic handling, going out to the swings and so on.

b   However, there may still be many times when he needs to have his anxieties allayed by hearing your voice. Apart from this, such children seem to feel much more secure if they get **firm, consistent handling**. Perhaps some of the activities in other parts of this book can be used to interest your child as an alternative to headbanging, attention seeking, reducing tension, screaming, over-activeness and remoteness. It is useful to experiment.

c   Provide plenty of interests and pleasurable experiences and relaxed attention. Make sure he has plenty of purposeful activities in which to gain pleasure and success, and lavish encouragement and praise for acceptable behaviour.

d   It seems that the most helpful method of approach is the natural one, whereby the child carries out everyday situations with an understanding person, with whom he can relate. This person, perhaps his mum, will within a fairly definite routine, help to remove fears about situations he probably feels to be threatening. Children need you to make a predictable environment for them. They need firm boundaries to be set so that they feel secure in their family life. They need cuddles, to be talked to, and people who are sensitive to their physical comfort, well-being and health.

The child who doesn't want to be handled

Some children react strongly to close handling. Some stiffen, arch their backs and scream, others just stiffen and slide away from you. Again, it is hard to know why this should be and reasons are likely to vary.

For example,

- the child has frequent bouts of colic and is often in pain. You can probably understand the discomfort of being handled during a violent tummy-ache. Consult your doctor about any suspected illness.

- visually impaired children who were premature or sickly babies, who have spent their early months in hospital and possibly in an incubator, will lack early physical contact or handling experience with their mothers. This is important to both mother and child and may, combined with the emotional experience for parents of having a child who has impaired vision, cause a breakdown in the physical relationship of the child with the mother. Later, whilst energetic physical play may be accepted, close physical contact may be rejected.

- some children disabled through maternal rubella in the early months of pregnancy, who are also early 'back archers', seem to dislike being handled; so do athetoid children and some hydrocephalic children with physical disabilities.

A few children appear to hate handling, making strong objection to anything being put into their hands, and withdraw them. It is usually the same children who hate change as if they are afraid of new things. Often there are just one or two things which they will accept. Here are a few ideas to help such a child to be more adventurous in his acceptance of new and unfamiliar playthings.

a Do not anticipate his displeasure by saying, 'He won't like that', or 'He only likes his bell rattle', and so on. Children are often good at fulfilling your expectations.

b Do not necessarily interpret a toy being dropped as disinterest. He may have been experimenting with its sound as it hit the floor, or he may have wanted you to return it to him. Try returning it to him a few times.

c Talk to him about the toy. Give it a name. Warn him that you are about to shake it or give it to him.

d Give him more control over the situation. For instance, sit him on your lap and draw up to a table. Put an object on the table, and, holding him at the elbow, help him to reach towards it, letting his hand touch it, or draw back, saying what you are doing.

e Leave a new toy beside his familiar and accepted ones so that **he** comes across it accidentally.

Gradually these children can begin to like being handled, starting with a routine of regular short periods and finding something about it which they learn to appreciate as they mature. In some cases, it has been found advantageous to 'flood' them with cuddling and caressing, ignoring the child's protests. Some children have eventually come to enjoy this kind of attention.

When you are attempting to introduce new toys, make the rest of the situation very familiar, and particularly caring and rewarding.

When he rejects a toy or activity the first time it is presented, keep introducing it for short periods at frequent intervals in play. This will help to lessen his fear of an unknown experience as his finger tips and muscles learn to anticipate the new sensations, which gradually become familiar and less threatening.

Dressing and undressing

We have discussed in Chapter 2 the reasons why visually impaired children need to be encouraged to use **both** hands together, to develop an awareness of self. The aim is to help each child to become as **competent** and autonomous as is possible, within any limitations imposed by the complexity of his disabilities. The importance of organisation and a predictable environment for visually impaired children has already been stressed. It is helpful if the same sequence of steps is followed each time something is being taught or practised. Remember, the aim is **to help the child to help himself** – not to do everything for him or anticipate all his needs.

a From the first encourage your child to take a positive part as you dress him, by expecting him for example, to raise an arm or leg appropriately on request. Undressing/dressing skills should only be taught at appropriate times, for example when a child goes to bed or gets up, goes to the toilet, goes swimming, goes outdoors, or on his return home/indoors.

b Remember to **talk** to your child about what he is doing – give him the words to suit the action! This verbal activity emphasises the association between the object (garment) and the activity he is performing, and so enables him to begin acquiring language concepts.

c The main skills needed for undressing, dressing, washing, cleaning teeth and brushing hair are:

- **knowing the parts of the body,** for example 'lift your **arm**', 'pull the vest over your **head**', 'fasten the zip to your **waist**', 'pull your socks up over your **ankles**'
- **head and trunk control and balance**, for example **lifting** one leg or arm at a time; **bending** forward; **twisting** the body to fasten side buttons or zips; **pushing** an arm through a sleeve; **pulling** socks up.
- **a degree of manipulative dexterity**, for example fine finger movements/pincer grip for buttons, button holes, zips, pop-fasteners, buckles, laces, toggles, and velcro; and an ability to hold one part of a garment steady in position, in order to pull on/off or fasten with the other hand.
- **knowledge of appropriate language**, for example left/ right, up/down, over/under, top/bottom, front/back, inside/outside, in/out, forwards/backwards, push/pull, lift/ drop, bend, press, tuck; and the names of different articles of clothing, for example vest, socks, shoes, pants, trousers, T-shirt, knickers, dress, ribbon, belt, coat, hat, and wellington boots.

d It is useful when dressing and undressing to break the process into small steps so that your child feels successful each time a step is completed.

e A blind child will need to learn the difference in **textures** of clothes, and distinguish one garment from another, and will need help to recognise whether the garment is inside out or back to front – therefore small but distinctive marks (such as embroidered cross-stitch or zig-zag) are helpful. These can be stitched at the neckline (or waist, back of sock), so that the child learns to locate them easily on each garment.

Begin with undressing which is easier than dressing. At first a child will just allow **you** to remove the whole garment for example a coat, without attempting to assist you.

Step 1. The first step is to encourage him (by manipulating his hands under yours, if necessary) to pull the coat off the end of one arm. You have removed **all** of the coat except for the remaining cuff – so his task is to pull it the last few inches/centimetres. Say: 'Take your coat off'. When he can do that step well, progress to the next.

Step 2. You remove all of the garment except for one whole sleeve which he takes off to the request, 'Take off your coat'.

Step 3. You pull the coat collar and lapels back over his shoulders. He reaches behind with his right hand to remove the left sleeve as well as doing Step 2.

Step 4. Drop the garment off his shoulders at the same time as he grasps the front edges of his coat then lifts the coat and wriggles his shoulders as he eases the garment backwards over them. Then he does Steps 3 and 2. He has now completely removed his coat.

A left-handed child may learn this the other way round.

It helps a child to learn more quickly if he practises using a rather loose coat or jacket.

Having achieved the removal of the coat encourage him to find the loop at the back and to put the loop over his own coat-hook (marked with a solid symbol such as a toy car), and to hang the garment **tidily**. **Organisation** and **routine** are particularly important for visually impaired children.

If your child is encouraged to lie or fold clothes with the back uppermost (remember that a distinctive embroidered X will be easy to find), this should lead, eventually, to him putting his clothes on correctly.

Your child needs a toothbrush, mug, face cloth, hairbrush, and towel. These should be kept in the same place. There should be a particular peg on which to hang outdoor coats and a place to keep his 'wellies'. In this way your child learns to live harmoniously with others and to develop the personal organisation which is so necessary for a visually impaired person's day to day living. It helps your child find things and orientate himself.

Each child is more satisfied and is happier with every skill that he masters. How to put on a T-shirt is an example of real skill.

The child must:
- choose his T-shirt from an ordered collection of clothes
- find the arm and neck holes
- find the back of the T-shirt
- check that it is the right way up and not inside out
- place first one arm then the other into the sleeves
- lift it over his head
- push his head through
- pull the T-shirt down
- if necessary tuck the bottom of T-shirt into trousers, or skirt.

In order to help him reach that degree of skill it will be necessary over a period of time to work backwards through the list adding each skill bit by bit.

This early organisation demands a great deal of patience on the part of the adult. Encouragement, praise, persistence, patience and time given to the child's acquisition of these skills ensure a solid foundation of social competence, pride in appearance and confidence and independence in adolescence and adult life.

a   Where a child also has a physical disability affecting his arms you must remember to teach him to put his weaker hand into the sleeve first. He may need to practise 'pushing down' with his thumb tucked inside a garment, helped by the other hand outside.

b   A physically disabled visually impaired child may find it easier to achieve independence in dressing if neck bands have elastic woven into the material, or a garment has a polo-neck.

c   He may cope more easily with trousers with elastic at the waist rather than buckles or buttons; or

d   Substitute velcro fastenings for buttons and zips.

e   A child who has physical disabilities may find it easier to dress or undress from a sitting or lying position.

Chapter 6

Everyday life

All children

Play is an important aspect of a young child's life and education. We know that **children learn through play**. It is the natural way for a child to get to know about her surroundings, the way things work and why they do so, and most important of all, the child learns about herself both as a person and in relation to other people.

Through play a child is given the opportunity to become competent in using her body; she learns to concentrate, to try out new ideas, to foster curiosity, thus exercising initiative, imagination, and creativity. Playing helps a child to acquire patience, to develop independence and self-confidence, to practise grown-up behaviour and to develop a sense of control over her world.

Language and play help a child to come to terms with incidents which are, perhaps, frightening to her. In reconstructing such an experience – perhaps a hospital visit, or maybe falling over out-of-doors – in her play and in verbalising or 'talking out' the sequence of events which occurred, the child is developing this sense of control over her environment, and learning to understand her fears and emotions.

A sighted child begins to create. She does so in a variety of ways – by building sandcastles, towers or bricks, making plasticine models, painting, creating models out of junk materials – all are ways of changing one medium or shape into another. Often, what is created by the child bears no resemblance to the adult's idea of that object, but the child has the opportunity to exercise imagination, use muscular skill, develop the ability to think and plan, and to learn basic facts about the particular material or combination of materials used in the construction.

By observing the child, adults can then support the child's learning and perhaps even extend it.

Visually impaired children

This chapter is about making the most of the everyday things you are involved in. As you begin to enjoy the playing you will probably find that you are beginning to see things about your child's progress that show little developments or signs of enjoyment in activities. The sections which follow will lead you further and further into enjoying and watching out for these, so that as you dip into different parts of the chapter you will be able to work out more easily what your child needs now – and you will be able to give the best education your child can have.

It is essential that a visually impaired child should have the opportunity to rearrange things in order to learn what parts make up the whole object, to learn about the weight, shape, size, movement, texture, and so on of each of those parts, and incidentally, to learn new words in association with them. Thus, a child's play will bring opportunities to broaden the experience of language.

It is also essential that a visually impaired child should, like sighted peers, be encouraged and helped to create things. What is created and what language is used to talk about what has been created will, of course, depend upon the experiences and the extent of early exploration.

All the activities you have enjoyed with your child will help her to learn to play. Everyday life allows children to be spontaneous – which is the essence of play.

Partnership activities involving everyday experiences

a   Encourage her to play with ice-cubes, or empty them into and out of a bowl. Put your cold hands onto her cheek. She will learn from this that there are some cold, wet, slippery things.

b   Put a warm towel, baby lotion, or oil, on her tummy or in the palms of her hands or onto her face.

c   Let her learn that different objects and textures feel different and are hot or cold, dry, wet, smooth, rough, soft, and so on. She needs to be given soft, hard, fuzzy and sticky objects to hold to learn about textures, their weight and temperature.

d   Pots and pans make excellent play materials and are 'natural' toys in addition to being easily available. They make excellent musical toys (cymbals and drums) and if brightly coloured clothes pegs are placed around the rim of the saucepans a child will enjoy grasping the pegs firmly to remove them all. This is a form of grasping which leads to even more refined hand use and more accurate hand-eye coordination.

e   Let her help you with simple household chores – it may encourage her to concentrate for longer periods if you sing together about your shared activities, for example 'This is the way I dust the chairs/sweep the floor/make my bed/clean the window...' Introduce your child to a feather duster or even a dustpan or handbrush (firm and soft), sponge, chamois leather (damp and dry), duster, nail brush and pan scourer.

f   Use transparent photograph 'corners' to attach pictures, shapes, or pieces or cellophane to the windows, so that she can look at or through them when the sun shines. This activity will add another dimension to her 'looking'.

g   A supply of large paper bags and sacks is useful as play material. Masks and hats can be made easily (and cheaply!). Hiding her face as a form of hide and seek or 'guess who?' is another idea, while crawling or being pushed through or inside the sack gives endless fun.

h Water play using small clockwork toys for hand-eye coordination development has been mentioned before. But water play in general with all kinds of utensils and objects for pouring, floating, dropping into the water, sailing on it is an essential element for every child. Be sure to include corks, pebbles, sticks, shells, leaves, string, and metal things.

i Give your child a box of different objects for rummaging in and exploring. You can include almost empty face cream jars, a metal teapot, old vinyl records, a hairbrush, paint brush, sieves, an old clock, vacuum cleaner hose, an egg whisk (not the rotary kind) and so on.

Imaginative, creative and imitative play

Imaginative play overlaps considerably with creative and imitative play. Children enjoy 'helping' with household chores – dusting, digging, feeding baby and washing the car. All are activities which help them to practise 'grown up' skills. From this stage sighted children move to the more complex stages of imaginative play where any object, utensil or dressing-up garment will spark off an idea and these items become what the child wishes them to be. Children will play out frightening or pleasant experiences; their world will be transformed – they are no longer in the lounge or bedroom in their thoughts; they may well be 'a firefighter with a helmet on rescuing a dog from the pet shop engulfed in thick grey smoke'. The object which set the children's imagination to work might well have been a sand bucket.

Old hats (men's and women's), handbags, adult shoes, gloves, baskets, shawls or scarves are all interesting materials to use in children's play.

All children develop self-confidence and specific motor skills through indulging in varied physical activities such as climbing, swinging on ropes or ladders, balancing, jumping, crawling, racing and swimming, to name but a few. Naturally, you will need to make sure that obstacles to be climbed or jumped upon are structurally sound. These activities help children towards play.

For a visually impaired child this important stage in development will depend greatly upon the opportunities she has had for direct experiences, the stories she has been told, the explanations which have been given in response to her incessant questions of 'What is that sound?', 'Why is there a funny smell?', 'What makes it work?' and so on.

At this stage too, miniature toys, such as dolls' furniture and dinky cars, are used by sighted children to create a different world. Such miniature toys mean very little to children with impaired vision, because for example, 'car' means the texture of the upholstery, the sound of the engine, the clicking of the indicators, and the smell of petrol. It is difficult to grasp the idea of a large metal shape in its entirety. They can be aware only of the small parts they touch separately with each hand as they explore the bodywork. They may have no concept of length, width, height or depth.

A visually impaired child will enjoy imaginative play equally as much as sighted peers if she is allowed to examine the rope ladder, the tree trunk or the balancing bars carefully, before being encouraged to play with materials. Like a sighted child, a visually impaired child will attempt normally only what she knows she can manage at a particular stage.

Many multi-disabled children will have restrictions imposed upon them by physical disability or delay in the development of their intellectual ability. Like their sighted peers, they too should be encouraged to:
- slide along benches
- crawl into boxes, barrels or tunnels
- stretch over from one box or chair to another
- balance on mats, bricks or tins as stepping stones
- pull themselves over one type of obstacle onto another at a different level

even when this means that the child's limbs may have to be manipulated to enable them to succeed. With praise for effort at every little stage successfully completed, a visually impaired child will be motivated to 'try again' and to achieve more.

Positive play

Play and learning for a child with disabilities then, whatever the difficulties, must be something that happens in an enjoyable, fun-filled atmosphere, where the adults show an optimistic, positive attitude towards the child. Children must learn that what they are doing, have done and will be doing is important; attitudes will play a major role in their successful development and knowledge of themselves. It is so important to have positive expectations of a child's abilities and performance. Remember that if you expect nothing from her, then a child will respond in a very negative way, making little or no effort, and progress will cease.

Magnetic toys

Some visually impaired children enjoy using magnetic materials in their play. There are many different kinds of magnetic toys available, such as the 'textured' shapes of magnetic memo holders, magnetic letters and figures, and pattern-making shapes. Older children who have stopped putting toys in their mouths will enjoy magnetic sculpture executive toys. One such toy called a 'magnetic nut tree' has proved very popular with numerous multi-disabled children. Magnetic fishing games, magnetic marbles, office shapes/planning indicators and so on, are readily available at a wide range of prices.

Magnetic toys help to reduce the frustrations which visually impaired children experience when their 'constructions' move and drop, scattering pieces everywhere, or are disturbed by the movements of others.

Ideas for toys

Recently, manufacturers have become more aware of the need to incorporate vibration and voiceboxes into many different kinds of toys. Although not necessarily designed with disabled children in mind, these are excellent playthings for any child. We have found that multi-disabled visually impaired children can enjoy controlling things such as toy make-up and nail care kits themselves and occasionally will show a degree of imaginative play through their use. There is a greater range of this type of toy commercially available now and, although expensive, these would be a good suggestion for a child's birthday or Christmas present from relatives or friends.

Electronic games and computer software can be excellent for developing specific skills, if carefully selected. However, it is important that these games and toys require some degree of effort on the part of the child if she is to be able at some stage to entertain herself. Electronic sounds can be very confusing and may distort a child's hearing and fine auditory discrimination if she is allowed to play with these items for long periods of time. She may also become 'addicted' to them and refuse to handle other play materials; so ration the times spent on them. If a child shows interest in one of these special electronic games, it can be a good idea to use the game as a helpful reward for effort in playing with other materials or toys.

Remember that most ordinary toys can now be adapted easily to take a variety of 'touch switches' which are specially designed for children with disabilities, so that precise hand/eye movements and increasing physical effort by the child can be rewarded in many more interesting and stimulating ways.

An interesting collection of materials for building can be acquired easily and cheaply if you use a little imagination to transform household 'junk'. Some examples are

- air-fresheners of different kinds (even when well sterilized many will still retain some of their fragrance!)
- knitting machine spools can be found in different sizes, shapes and colours
- plastic funnels and sprinkler bottles
- foam rubber pieces of different thicknesses; a bag of off-cuts of wood (wedges, rectangles, rings and so on) from a local carpenter is very interesting because of the smell and smoothness or roughness of the wood – it makes a change from plastic
- corks of various sizes and shapes, mats, bottle corks, storage jar corks, tiles of different thicknesses
- lengths of plastic tubing to straddle across cones, corks and wedges, or through wooden rings, are also interesting to use.

There is a wide range of toys of all kinds suitable for sighted children which if carefully selected with your child's abilities in mind, will prove useful for helping her to acquire a specific skill at the stage when she is ready for it.

Shared fun times help to develop your relationship with your child and to build up communication skills. Objects, activities or experiences which she enjoys can be used as rewards, and anything that works, however unusual must be used to the child's advantage. It is important that a good combination and variety of activities is provided, for this allows your child to develop in a variety of ways. Experiences that are repeated and are varied and stimulating, can be used to help your child increase awareness of her own body, her actions, of her surroundings and of the people in her world. These experiences help her to integrate or interpret all that the senses of touch, smell, hearing, taste and sight tell her.

The importance of play

Studies of the language development of visually impaired multi-disabled children all indicate the enormity of the problems which can beset these children – lack of real first-hand experience, anxiety, disordered perceptions about people and objects in their environment, inability to organise or interpret their experiences, thoughts, feelings, needs or desires. Their 'world' is at the end of their fingertips, and if they cannot use their hands purposefully and they are immobile, then naturally their world is limited.

All children need to develop autonomy and entertain themselves in a constructive way. We try to encourage multi-disabled children to become independent in feeding, dressing, washing and bathing and so on, and sometimes as they play they will need to learn to amuse themselves; if this can be through constructive means, all the better. From time to time a child, like an adult, needs some time to herself 'doing her own thing', even if that is not a very productive activity. We all need to learn to strike the right balance between direction, structure and withdrawal.

Remember that when there is nothing interesting to do, your child might begin rocking, eye-poking, light-gazing or finger/hand flapping. All children tend to return to comfort behaviours such as thumb-sucking when they don't want outside stimulation. Their bodies stimulate them and are their world. However, keep alert so that your child does not use these behaviours all the time when there is not a need for comfort or relaxation. Provide interesting things to interact with and encourage your child to use them. At each stage of this essential play experience, a child may be stimulated mentally as well as physically; she is able to perfect a number of different skills, she is able to develop self-confidence, she is increasing her vocabulary, and her command of language may be widened and made more purposeful through every activity. Every situation provides an opportunity for language building, and deliberate attempts should be made to see that your child has experience with the language of the body, of space, shape, size, length, weight, texture, heat, movement and so on.

Activities to encourage vocalising

a At the baby stage, let your child feel your mouth as you talk or play games of talking on her cheek or making repetitive sounds like 'baa-baa-baa'.

b Copy any simple attempts your child makes at vocalising. Sometimes this can develop into a sort of conversation in voiced sounds.

c Introduce animal noises. Sometimes these amuse a child so much that she may attempt to reproduce them.

d She may enjoy making noises with her head in an upturned bucket, resting sideways on the floor. Not all children will take to this however.

e Put a balloon against her cheek and talk through it.

f Put a balloon between her hands and against her mouth. Play at making noises from your side or encourage her to feel the strange sensation on her lips as she makes a sound.

g Rest her hands or hand on a musical box as it plays.

h When you move a playing musical box a little way from her, move one of her arms from the elbow to put a hand down on it again.

i   Once she is reaching to grasp toys, shake one of her rattles to her left or her right and help her to be successful in finding them.

j   When she is lying down, drop a toy beside one ear, then the other, and help her to roll over to touch it.

k   When she is lying down, play a musical box beside one ear or the other and help her to roll over to touch it. By holding her arm at the elbow, direct her hand to where it is.

l   If she has even the smallest bit of sight, try to use toys that have both sound and visual appeal.

m   When two adults are playing with her, one calls 'Come here... '(use her name) whilst the other adult moves her towards the voice.

n   Again whilst still playing with two adults, one sounds a tambourine or a tinkly ball at a short distance, saying, 'Here you are!' and the other adult helps to move her to find the sound source.

o   Put a playing musical box or radio in one place or in a room and help her move to find it, saying 'Where is the ... ? Let's find it.'

p   Call to her from different rooms in the house, saying where you are. Call to her from along the street when your partner has charge of her.

q   If your kitchen has a hard floor, construct a simple square pen with large boxes. Let your child sit inside to drop or throw a ping pong ball, listen to it bouncing and try to retrieve it.

r   Roll an electronic bleeping ball around and let her find it, or, if she cannot move much, help her.

s   If a child is interested in making voiced, lip or tongue sounds, copy her and try to organise a sort of 'sound' conversation. Try to introduce rhythms into it, and, whilst your child may imitate some sounds, you try to introduce fresh ones in the middle of the game.

t Give her cardboard cylinders (from inside a roll of tin foil, toilet rolls and so on). Encourage her to blow and hum into them.

u Play at blowing down straws or rubber or plastic tubing into a large bottle of water or blowing into a whistle or trumpet.

v Visually impaired children enjoy rhymes and songs the same as other children. Some children who have additional disabilities seem to respond to certain tunes with pleasurable vocalisation. Acknowledge these sounds.

w Some children produce tunes quite accurately without the words. Others remember the words but not the tune. Children in general seem to be stimulated into vocalising during cosy sessions on a one-to-one basis, whereby songs and tunes and little singing games are shared in an intimate atmosphere. (CDs and tapes have a real place but are **not** a substitute for such times of sharing, unless you listen and perhaps sing along to them together.)

x Surprising interest and response is sometimes shown when names, requests and questions are put to well-known tunes. Some children who do not speak normally have been known to vocalise relevantly in song.

y Use a length of venting hose from an old tumble dryer to encourage your child to vocalise into one end and listen through the other.

Language

All children

Sighted children pick up some language incidentally through seeing what is being talked about. Without vision a child may hear but not necessarily know what is being talked about. Words or sounds may have very little, or distorted, meaning. For this reason, it is vital that events should be experienced at first hand as far as possible, accompanied by appropriate language and having things named. It is good if parents chat to their child right from the beginning when they wash, change, dress and feed their child.

When a child is unresponsive this is hard to remember to do and may appear to sound odd, but it is worth persevering.

A baby who is able to engage in eye contact with her parents, relatives, friends or a stranger whilst she smiles or babbles, is likely to encourage a response of smiling or talking from the adult. A visually impaired baby may drop her head or 'still' to listen to people around her. She is unable to engage them in eye contact and may not so much as turn towards them. People may conclude that she is not interested in them and her parents may have to be bold enough to explain that she really does like people to talk directly to her.

A sighted youngster reaches a stage when she points at things which fascinate her, but which are beyond her reach. Parents respond in a variety of ways, but almost always with accompanying speech, perhaps naming the object. Pointing is a sighted response which many visually impaired babies do not do. They may not know of the exact whereabouts of personal treasures until they are able to go to find them themselves, or ask.

Not only does a visually impaired child have less opportunity for incidental learning but until she gets moving in some fashion she is restricted in discovering what is around and what everything is called.

You cannot foresee how much language an individual child will acquire. Much also depends on her general ability and the severity of any other disabilities. It is certain that, if and when it comes, her language understanding will come first. She will learn to use language later on as a means of getting the things she wants.

Communication

The sort of understanding needed for communication will not grow in a child until her world begins to make some sense to her and she develops an inner language.

Some children take a very long time to **find their own identity** and real meaning in their world. Some of them may learn to speak and find pleasure in it, but have difficulty in **using speech to influence** their world even by asking for simple needs to be fulfilled. They may continue to repeat or 'parrot' speech they hear around them beyond the normal time, or even know parts of nursery rhymes word for word, but not use speech to communicate, rather they use it as a form of play.

Some of these children may appear to be moving around aimlessly repeating simple activities. Some may remain in their own inner world and not wish to venture outside it. These children **may also resist being communicated with.**

Bear in mind that unexpected touches, knocks, sounds and communications are less easy to interpret without sight. A child may need to be reassured about people approaching and leaving. Unless you say her name **first** to attract her attention, she may not know that you are speaking to her. She may not be sure whether someone has left the room unless they say 'Laura(name), I'm going now. Goodbye.' She will be happier if she is warned before being touched and she will need to have answered questions such as, 'Who was that?', 'What is happening?' and 'What is going on?', when she hears unfamiliar sounds and voices. She may be upset by an angry voice and think she is at fault, unless the 'guilty' person is named first.

Partnership activities to encourage your child to communicate

a   Sing your child's name on two or more notes.

b   Clap in rhythm to her name and the names of family members and other children around.

c   Sing everyday commands or questions.

d   If your child is small, hold her and dance with her to music.

e   If your child is small, put her on your knee and sway or bounce her to tunes and rhymes. Let each song have a distinctive movement which she learns to expect.

f Move rhythmically to music with a strong beat by clapping, stamping, or tapping.

g Tap out rhythms of names or words as you say them.

h Copy rhythm patterns. The adult does this alternately with the child, one beat first, then two, gradually devising more complicated rhythms.

Body language, gestures and facial expression

Young children and adults often show us what they want to say through the way they move their bodies. It is wonderful when a multi-disabled visually impaired child somehow conveys by movements of her body that she wants to be swung or jumped. You know she is aware of what is going on and wants to take part.

We need to develop body language plus touch clues alongside the spoken word, as this expands communication. However, it will be important to study your child to decide whether you are making life too easy for her so that she does not have to produce words. If that seems to be so, then praising what she does is more productive than criticism. Build her confidence and help her to feel positively about herself. If a child has a hearing loss as well, you may need to use some form of sign communication. There are several publications available which discuss this issue and make practical suggestions. One of the organisations representing the interests of deaf people, such as the National Deaf Children's Society or Sense may also be able to help.

Partnership activities to encourage communication by gesture

a Play singing games with your child, such as 'See Saw Marjorie Daw', holding her hands and swaying her on your knee. Pause to give her opportunity to move her body to 'ask' for more.

b When playing 'Round and Round the Garden' or tickling games, notice if she positions her hand or body in readiness for further 'goes'.

c When you greet her, for instance when returning from work, say 'Hello' and put her hands on your face. Look forward to a time when you position yourself and wait for her to place her hands on your face in greeting.

d Watch out for lip and tongue movements which may indicate thirst.

e Notice small movements of hands, arms or feet, or changes in facial expression which appear to be showing a pleasure reaction.

f Play tickling rhymes with a very dramatic, perhaps noisy, build up to a tickle. Give her time to show her anticipation by noises, facial expression or movement.

g Find 'her sound' and the sounds of other family members on a toy organ. Introduce a fun element by varying pitch, tone and rhythm.

h If a child vocalises, copy her to try to get an alternate pattern.

Using everyday situations

Whilst it is a good idea to put aside a short time each day to do 'special' things with your child, such as those suggested in this book, everyday activities can be used to develop your child's awareness and understanding.

What can I see?

Reflection, contrast.
Opportunity for fixating.
Opportunity for tracking.
Hand-eye coordination.

Everyday life – joining in

Licking.
Tasting a variety of food.
Sorting cutlery & china.
Handling.
Removing and fitting lids.
Hanging up tea-towels and hand towels.
Squeezing dishcloth.
Wiping table.
Drying dishes.
Safety considerations.

My body

Position and support.
Movement: head, reaching, pushing/pulling
Space: height, level, distances, position of objects.
Feeling:
    Pots and pans, spoons, ingredients.
Manipulating:

holding	chopping	turning (tap)
feeling inside	cutting	shaking
tipping	patting	switching
filling	pinching	screwing
stirring	sieving	spreading
spooning	rolling	

Communicating

Sounds:
    Food mixer
    Chopping
    Mixing
    Pots and pans
    Water running
    Swishing
    Ingredients of different smells,
    flavours, textures.
    Weighing – heavy, light.
    Oven – temperature – smell.
    Liquids.

Being with other people

Shared experience to build relationship.
Success and failure.
Experiment and mastery.
Observance of safety rules and instruction.
Learning about their own reactions, for
example revulsion, withdrawal, pleasure.
Self-awareness, self-esteem

COOKING

Learning/understanding

Space.
Permanence of objects.
Learning how food gets to the table.
Association between texture, tastes and smells.
Weight, size, textures, smell, shape, volume,
sounds, (of materials, and of individuals).
Liquids and how they behave.
Changes in ingredients from raw to cooked,
from hot to cold, varying nature of ingredients,
such as an egg whole or broken.

Experiencing

Smelling: ingredients.
Listening: mixing, chopping, clinking, swishing.
Feeling: plastic, metal, wood, china, liquids and
solids, warm, cold, icy, large and small ingredients'
consistencies, such as custard, egg white.
Tasting: sweet, sour, spicy, bitter, hot, salty, crunchy,
smooth, chewy, biteable, lickable, suckable.

Partnership activities: baking

a   Pat your child's hands on the boxes and bags of baking ingredients. Bring them near her nose to smell if she cannot do so herself.

b   Help her to shake the sugar, currants, salt, in their containers to see what different sounds they make. (The containers themselves will have interesting sounds too, such as bags, jars, boxes, tins.) Help her to put a finger inside and to taste the contents.

c   Put a spoon into her hand and help her turn it around in the mixing bowl. Listen to its sound. Smell and taste.

d   Feel inside the baking tins, bang on them, and listen to them being put down on the table.

e   Help her scoop up some mixture and 'plop' it into the baking tin.

f   Tell her what you are doing as you open and close the oven door.

g   Tell her to listen for the timer. Set it to ring when the baking is done.

h   When finished and it is cool enough, let her handle, crumble and taste the finished product.

Look for the sound potential in other seemingly humdrum household activities, and when you find an opportunity, think of ways your child may join in.

A visit to the shops

The following section provides ideas for making the most of a visit to the shops.

a   Tell your child that you are going to the shops. Tell her what the weather is like, and which coat if any to wear. Go with her to find her coat. Help her to put it on, encouraging her to do as much as she can. Talk to her about the type of buttons and what they feel like. Count them as you do them up or count with her as she does them up. Listen to the sound of a zip, poppers or velcro.

b Sit her in her buggy. Talk to her as you do up the harness. Ask her if she is comfortable, and talk to her about putting her feet on the foot rest.

c Check out loud that you have your purse, keys, bags. Let her feel each of these as you name them.

d Let the child feel the door and door handle as you go out. Listen to it bang shut, and the key turning in the lock.

e Draw your child's attention to the sound of the buggy's wheels on the ground. Give the noise a name and say it over and over, for example 'bumpety bump'.

f Meeting a neighbour or noticing a dog bark are important experiences for all children. Watch your child closely so that you can tell when she has heard a noise that she wants you to interpret. It might be the sound of milk bottles being delivered or the electric whine of a milk float. A motorbike going past has a distinctive sound, as has a bus or lorry. You can use language to imitate these sounds. Children often find these sounds more amusing than 'real' words and are a good way of getting them interested in language and communication.

g Some children enjoy trailing their hands outside the buggy. You might push the buggy so that your child can feel a soft (not prickly) hedge.

h Talk to your child as you bump down kerbs, and as you tip the buggy to go back up the kerb on the other side of the road.

i As you go along tell your child where you are going. Some shops which you pass will have a distinctive smell such as a bakery or a florist's, chip shop or take-away.

j The supermarket has lots of sounds and smells to remark on. Your child can feel the wire basket, and perhaps flap the handle back and forth before you begin shopping.

k If you have time you can let your child handle some of the items you choose. Packets of cereal can be shaken to make a satisfying noise. Packets of pasta crinkle loudly. Tins feel heavy. Washing powder has a strong smell. Refrigerated items are cold to touch. Toilet rolls are bulky and yet light. Handling all these things helps your child to build up a clearer picture of the world.

l   Some fruit and vegetables can be handled, offering a wide variety of skins to feel. Some also have pleasant distinctive smells such as melons or strawberries.

m   Many supermarkets now bake bread on the premises. You could break a small roll open for your child at the counter, associating the taste with the warmth and smell.

n   The fish counter also has an obvious smell – though you may understandably draw the line at your child smelling of fish all the way home!

o   Waiting at the checkout can make even the most relaxed adult feel impatient. Children have often run out of patience by this point in the trip. You can use this time to explore together what is in the basket or trolley. Your child might also listen to the barcode scanner bleeping as the checkout assistant runs each item of shopping over the light to register it on the till. Some tills make noises as the receipt is printed out, or a cheque or credit card slip is inserted.

p   Lighting in supermarkets is often quite bright, and some children will find pleasure in gazing up at the ceiling lights.

q   It can be a good idea to return home a slightly different way to add interest to the journey. Perhaps the return trip can include going under a railway bridge or in a subway that echoes. You can listen together to the cars and lorries as you wait to cross the road. You might use a pelican crossing, helping your child to push the button, to feel the bumpy pavement and the bleep of the green man telling you that it is safe to cross.

r   Or you might go back via a park which gives a respite from traffic noise. As you push the buggy over grass or on a gravel path the movement will feel different to your child. Talk about this. You might hear children playing, and the regular groan of swings going back and forth. A see-saw and children climbing the iron steps of a slide all offer sounds for interpretation.

s   If you are doing a big shop, you might go by car. It's important to give names to all the experiences this involves. In the car, there is the click as you fasten safety belts and car seat harnesses. Starting the engine, the noise of the motor and the ticking of the indicators can be commented on. Going into reverse gear to get into a parking space can be explained to your child.

t   On the bus, there are steps to climb to get on. Money has to be given to the driver, and a ticket received in return. You might sit near a window and let your child feel the vibration of the engine as it shakes the whole bus. The stopping and starting sensations give an opportunity for more talk. The seat can be interesting to feel; the cold metal pole and the furry seat fabric. The bell to indicate you want the next stop is often a favourite with children.

u   Arriving home with the bags of shopping you can repeat the process of letting your child help you to open the door. Some children may help put the shopping away. There is lots to talk about in terms of getting the cold shopping into the fridge or freezer before it thaws and why different things go in different places.

v   After all that, it must be time to put the kettle on!

If we analyse what has happened during an outing to the shops we discover how to take full advantage of everything that has happened. If we put things into chart form we also see the interconnections between every area of the learning experience.

Communication and language

Parent speaks to child about events.
Child's non-verbal responses encouraged.
Child's initiating sounds encouraged.
Opportunities given for anticipation.
Response to request.

Having fun

Happy response,
self-confidence.

Autonomy

Getting dressed by herself,
feeling food, keys, purse
and so on.

Opportunities for learning

Being part of everyday life

Self-esteem. Child included in everything. Child's responses acknowledged. Mastery increasing. Security, routine. Experience of meeting other children and adults. Experience of animals.

Real experiences

Listening to sounds and voices acknowledged and encouraged.
To feel sound and rhythm, texture, temperature, firmness, height and so on.
Smelling food, people, shops.
Tasting food.

Competent moving about

Positioning. Head control.
Body control – dressing, reaching, touching.

Getting around

Ground surfaces, shop smells, door, letter box.

Where next?

Parents and teachers of visually impaired children with additional disabilities always try to ensure that children develop their individual abilities to the full. This means teaching them to become aware of themselves, of their immediate surroundings and of the wider world; encouraging children to use all their senses as they explore their environment and learn to communicate with others.

The information and ideas in this book are drawn from many years of experience and are designed to act as a resource. We know that you will want to add many more ideas from your own experience in bringing up and teaching your visually impaired child.

We hope this book, which focuses on the early years, will be a helpful starting point for you and your child as a source of ideas for enjoyment, learning and having fun together.

Appendix A

Further reading

Unless otherwise indicated, all the publications below are available from:

RNIB Education Information Service
224 Great Portland Street
LONDON W1N 6AA

Tel: 0171-388 1266

100 popular toys and games for blind and partially sighted children (1994) 22 page catalogue produced jointly by the British Toy and Hobby Association and RNIB. Free. Print and braille.

Benefits for visually impaired children (1994) 4 page factsheet giving details of social security benefits, who qualifies for them and how to apply. Free. Print, braille and tape.

RNIB Book Sales Service Catalogue This annual catalogue provides titles and brief descriptions of books about visual impairment published in other countries in English which can be purchased through RNIB. Free. Print.

Getting started (1995) A guide to understanding your child's eye condition, how the eye works, some of the people who can help and language that you might come across. Priced. Print and tape.

One step at a time (1995) gives practical tips and advice for parents of a visually impaired baby. Priced. Print and tape.

Helping your visually impaired child (1994) 32 page booklet providing an introduction to the key services for blind and partially sighted children and their families. Priced (free to parents). Print and tape.

Music and visually impaired children (1991) 32 page booklet of advice for teachers. Priced. Print.

New directions (1990) A 48 page report considering the needs of multi-disabled visually impaired children and their families. Priced. Print.

Objects of Reference (1994) 32 page booklet promoting communication skills and concept development with visually impaired children who have other disabilities. Priced. Print.

Special schools for visually impaired children in the UK (1994) Free. Print and large print.

Useful books for parents and professionals working with visually impaired children (1993) A three page factsheet listing books supplied by RNIB and others. Free. Print.

VITAL *information* Collection of articles about visually impaired children with multiple disabilities put together by VITAL, the curriculum support group for professionals working with multiply disabled visually impaired children. Priced. Print and braille.

What shall we do to help? (1992) 16 page guide for mainstream nursery and playgroup leaders caring for visually impaired children. Priced. Print.

You and your sight: living with a sight problem (1994) 148 page guide giving practical advice and information to everyone with a serious sight problem. Published by HMSO. Priced. Print, tape and braille. Available from HMSO Publications Centre, PO Box 276, London SW8 5DT. Tel: 0171-873 9090.

Videos

The world in our hands (1993) Five videos with supporting booklets about blind babies and pre-school children. Priced. Available singly or as a complete set. Available from RNIB Book Sales Service, Garrow House, 190 Kensal Road, London W10 5BT. Tel: 0181-968 8600.

One of the family (1995) Four videos with supporting booklets about multi-disabled blind or partially sighted babies and children. Available singly or as a complete set. Available from RNIB Book Sales Service, Garrow House, 190 Kensal Road, London W10 5BT. Tel: 0181-968 8600.

Magazines and journals

eye contact The journal for parents and professionals involved in the eduction of visually impaired children who have additional learning difficulties. Published each school term by RNIB Education Information Service. Annual subscription.

Visability Published each school term by RNIB Education Information Service, this journal is for parents and professionals concerned with the education of visually impaired children. Each issue includes news on National Curriculum developments, books, courses, art, technology and leisure. Annual subscription.

Talking sense Quarterly magazine published by Sense (The National Deafblind and Rubella Association) Annual subscription. Tel: 0171-272 7774.

Information exchange Published three times a year. A magazine of ideas for parents and professionals relating to the needs of multiply disabled children with hearing and visual impairments. Tel: 0161-486 6514. Charge per issue.

Appendix B

RNIB services for children

RNIB runs over 70 different services for blind and partially sighted children and adults. Our services are also open to families of visually impaired people and to professionals working with them.

The following services are based at our head office:

RNIB, 224 Great Portland Street, London W1N 6AA
Tel: 0171-388 1266

- RNIB Education Information Service
- RNIB Benefit Rights and Information Team
- RNIB Health Service Development Unit
- RNIB Reference Library

If you have particular questions and are not sure which RNIB service to contact start with the RNIB Education Information Service. The team will be happy to answer your questions or put you in touch with a colleague who can help.

RNIB Education Centres

We also have five Education Centres which offer information, advice, training and specialist technology:

RNIB Education Centre: London, Garrow House, 190 Kensal Road
London W10 5BT   Tel: 0181-968 8600

RNIB Education Centre: Scotland, 10 Magdala Crescent
Edinburgh EH12 5BE   Tel: 0131-313 1876

RNIB Education Centre: North of England, Grosvenor House,
Grosvenor Road, Headingley, Leeds LS6 2DZ   Tel: 0113-274 8855

RNIB Education Centre: Midlands, c/o RNIB New College Worcester
Whittington Road, Worcester WR5 2JX   Tel: 01905-357635

RNIB Education Centre: Wales, 4th Floor, 33-35 Cathedral Road, Cardiff, CF1 2HB   Tel: 01222-668606

In addition we run the following specialist services:

RNIB Advocacy Service for parents
c/o RNIB Education Centre: Midlands

RNIB Curriculum Support Service
c/o RNIB Education Centre: Midlands

RNIB Integration Support Service
c/o RNIB Education Centre: North of England

RNIB Music Education Advisory Service
c/o RNIB Education Centre: London

RNIB Technology Education Advisory Service
c/o RNIB Education Centre: London

RNIB schools

RNIB runs six schools for visually impaired children. Details are given below of our four schools for younger children.

RNIB Sunshine House School Northwood in Middlesex provides specialist residential and day education and care for blind and partially sighted children aged from two to eight years old. The children have a wide range of abilities including those able to compete with sighted children in National Curriculum subjects and those who need coordinated, skilled help to develop their potential.
Tel: 01923-822538

RNIB Sunshine House School Southport provides specialist day and weekly residential education and support for children aged from two to eight who have a visual impairment. The children have additional disabilities affecting their movement, hearing, speech, understanding learning or behaviour. The school also offers short term assessments in physiotherapy, communication, and eating and drinking.
Tel: 01704-567174

RNIB Sunshine House School East Grinstead in West Sussex provides specialist residential education for children between 4 and 10 years old. The children are visually impaired and have additional disabilities affecting their movement, speech, understanding, learning and behaviour. All are developmentally delayed to a considerable degree and need individual care to acquire the most basic skills.
Tel: 01342-323141

RNIB Rushton Hall School in Northamptonshire is for boys and girls aged from 5 to 12 who are not only visually impaired but who have other disabilities as well, affecting their learning, movement, hearing, speech, ability to communicate or behaviour.
Tel: 01536-710506

Dryden House is based at RNIB Rushton Hall School and offers education and care for up to 2 weeks of the year for children in the age range 5-19 years.
Tel: 01536-710506

Forest House also based at RNIB Rushton Hall School offers independent all-round assessments and can make specific recommendations and suggest ways of working for your child's future development.
Tel: 01536-710506

All RNIB schools provide a further range of services within the area they serve, such as respite care, practical advice and suppport, parent days, toy libraries etc. For more information about these or other RNIB schools please contact the Schools Liaison Officer, RNIB Education, Training and Employment Division.
Tel: 0171-388 1266 ext 2272

Specialist products

RNIB Customer Services sells a wide range of specialist products for use by people with impaired vision. Over 600 items are described in six large print, tape or braille, easy reference product guides:

- Daily living
- Clocks and watches
- Games and puzzles
- Braille
- Learning
- Mobility

RNIB Customer Services, PO Box 173, Peterborough PE2 6WS. Tel: 0345-023153 (for the price of a local call)

RNIB Talking Book Service is a library service for blind and partially sighted people offering nearly 10,000 unabridged books on tape.
Tel: 0345-626843 (for the price of a local call)

Useful addresses

ACE (Advisory Centre for Education Ltd) 1B Aberdeen Studios, 22 Highbury Grove, London N5 2EA   Tel: 0171-354 8318/8321

Contact a Family,170 Tottenham Court Road, London W1P 0HA   Tel: 0171-383 3555

Council for Disabled Children, 8 Wakley Street London WC1V 7QU   Tel: 0171-843 6000

Family Welfare Association, 501-505 Kingsland Road, Dalston, London E8 4AU   Tel: 0171-254 6251

LOOK, The National Federation of Families with Visually Impaired Children, Queen Alexandra College, Court Oak Road, Harborne, Birmingham B17 9TG   Tel: 0121-428 5038

Mencap, 123 Golden Lane, London EC1Y 0RT   Tel: 0171-454 0454

National Children's Bureau, 8 Wakley Street London WC1V 7QU   Tel: 0171-843 6000

The National Deaf Children's Society 45 Hereford Road, London W2 5AH   Tel: 0171-229 9272

National Library for the Blind, Cromwell Road Bredbury, Stockport, SK6 2SG   Tel: 0161-494 0217

Playmatters/National Association of Toy and Leisure Libraries, 68 Churchway, London NW1 1LT   Tel: 0171-387 9592

Research Centre for the Education of the Visually Handicapped, Faculty of Education, University of Birmingham, PO Box 363, Birmingham B15 2TT — Tel: 0121-414 6733

RNIB, 224 Great Portland Street, London W1N 6AA — Tel: 0171-388 1266

Sense (National Deafblind and Rubella Association) 11-13 Clifton Terrace, London N4 3SR — Tel: 0171-272 7774

Scope (formerly Spastics Society), 12 Park Crescent, London W1N 4EQ — Tel: 0171-636 5020

VITAL (RNIB/VIEW Curriculum group for professionals working with multiply disabled visually impaired children) RNIB Rushton Hall School, Rushton, nr. Kettering, Northamptonshire NN14 1RR — Tel: 01536-710506